PIMP YOUR

NOODLES

First published in Great Britain in 2021 by Seven Dials
an imprint of The Orion Publishing Group Ltd
Carmelite House, 50 Victoria Embankment
London EC4Y 0DZ

An Hachette UK Company

3 5 7 9 10 8 6 4 2

Publisher: Vicky Eribo
Editor: Ru Merritt
Photography: Andrew Hayes-Watkins
Food Styling: Katy McLellean
Art Direction: Lucie Stericker
Design: Julyan Bayes
Production: Claire Keep

A CIP catalogue record for this book is
available from the British Library.
ISBN (Hardback) 978 1 8418 8425 7
ISBN (eBook) 978 1 8418 8426 4
Printed in China

www.orionbooks.co.uk

PIMP YOUR

NOODLES

OVER 60 KICK-ASS RECIPES FOR A DELICIOUS DINNER

SARAH COOK

CONTENTS

INTRODUCTION 1

FIVE FAST SALAD DRESSINGS 12

FIVE TASTY TOPPINGS 14

SUPER EASY 10-MINUTE FIXES 16

FRESH SALADS 26

SIZZLING STIR FRIES 42

SOULFUL SOUPS 58

COMFORTING CURRIES 72

PIMP TO THE MAX SPECIALS 88

INDEX 104

INTRODUCTION

Let's talk about noodles! Cheap and cheerful, they're a staple the world over, but particularly in South-east Asian cookery where they provide the perfect balance to some of the more fiery and gutsy ingredients used. It's their humble nature, though, that makes them so versatile, equally good in veg-packed, zingily dressed summer salads as they are in spoon-slurping, deep bowls of fragrant hot broth. Whether you're a noodle novice or pro cook, there's something for everyone in this collection.

Get ready to reinvent your midweek staples with simple, speedy options that need little more than a well-stocked store cupboard. Opt for authentic and unusual flavour combinations to wow friends with when you're entertaining, and nourish your body and your soul with super-green healthy offerings. The noodle know-how guide overleaf will show you how to choose, cook and serve the perfect option for any occasion – and the tips for filling your store cupboard will make future supermarket trips a breeze. Get inspired to jazz up your own creations with the easy pimps for toppings and dressings, or turn straight to the Super-easy chapter if you simply need something straightforward and tasty on the table in minutes. This book offers a solution to any mealtime dilemma.

Fine Wheat Noodles

Thick Wheat Noodles

HOW TO CHOOSE

Chinese wheat and egg noodles

Sold in supermarkets dried or as a straight-to-wok variety, these come in three sizes – thick, medium and fine – and you can also get egg-enriched versions. This is the broadest category of noodles and an Asian store will usually stock a dizzying array of 'mein', as these noodles are loosely known in Chinese cookery.

GOOD FOR stir-fries, soups and experimenting.
Try Corn & coriander noodle cakes (see page 93).

Medium Wheat Noodles

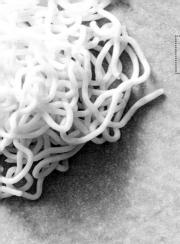

**Medium Wheat Noodles
(Straight-to-Wok)**

Butternut Squash Noodles

Vegetable noodles

Not exactly a noodle as such, but spiralised vegetables are all
the rage and a good accompaniment, or alternative, to regular noodles.
Try courgetti, 'boodles' (butternut squash), plus carrot, sweet potato and
even beetroot. Spiralising gadgets are fairly good value now, or look
for ready-prepared varieties in the supermarket.

GOOD FOR stir-fries and vitamin boosts. Try Curried
coconut noodle bowls (see page 82).

Courgette Noodles

Wide Udon Dried Noodles

Udon noodles

Fat and chewy, the fresh variety boasts a superior texture over dried – but you can buy dried wide udon and frozen udon now. Made from wheat flour, water and salt, these are the thickest of the Japanese noodles and are usually served in a broth.

GOOD FOR Japanese curries, soups and saucy stir-fries. Try Fish finger katsu udon (see page 75).

Soba noodles

This is another common Japanese noodle, traditionally served cold in salads. They are a distinctive brown colour, with a nutty flavour and slightly chewy texture, due to the addition of buckwheat flour. They are often prone to gumminess, so always rinse well (see How to cook, on page 8.

GOOD FOR salads and entertaining. Try Roast sweet potato & salmon salad with noodles (see page 39).

Udon Noodles (Straight-to-Wok)

Instant Noodles

Ramen and instant noodles

Another Japanese favourite, the word 'ramen' refers to a dish as well as a noodle type. They can be made with both egg and wheat flour, so colours can vary from white to yellow, and are often associated with instant noodles – packaged in single portions alongside sachets of flavourings to add to soups. However, their many varieties, from thin to thick, curly to straight, mean they are much more versatile.

GOOD FOR soups and broths. Try Full English ramen with bacon broth (see page 69).

Soba Noodles

Thin Brown Rice Noodles

Rice noodles

Like wheat, rice noodles come in an almost endless number of varieties and as their flavour is fairly bland, they are good for adding to boldly flavoured dishes. They're most commonly used in Thai and Vietnamese cookery – cuisines that favour strong and fragrant ingredients, such as chilli and fish sauce. Familiar types include brown varieties, vermicelli and dried flat 'ribbon' – the standard noodles for pad thai. Be careful not to confuse these with the wheat variety which are opaque and whiter in colour.

GOOD FOR salads, soups and dry stir-fries. Try Crowd-pleasing pad thai and Bang bang chicken summer rolls (see pages 45 and 90).

Thick Brown Rice Noodles

Vermicelli Noodles

**Green Tea
Vermicelli Noodles**

**Dried Ribbon
Wheat Noodles**

Glass noodles

Also known as cellophane noodles, these are so fine they're almost threadlike, and get the name from their transparent appearance after cooking. Made from any starch other than wheat or rice, mung bean, tapioca and sweet potato varieties are all common. Their unique texture and ability to soak up liquid make them a good choice in sharply dressed salads.

GOOD FOR soups and salads. Try Thai som tam salad (see page 31).

Glass Noodles

HOW TO COOK

Just like with Italian pasta, you usually don't want to overcook noodles, and where you look for an 'al dente' finish with spaghetti, most noodles should also still have a little 'bite'.

Dried wheat and egg noodles are fairly sturdy, so boiling is a good, quick option, whereas the straight-to-wok and fresh varieties of these will only require reheating in a microwave or pan. Depending on their type and thickness, most dried varieties will cook in 3–6 minutes in a saucepan of water that has already come to the boil. Salting the water isn't usually necessary as noodles often contain more salt than dried pasta, and are also often paired with salty accompaniments like soy sauce or miso.

Rice noodles cook even faster than the wheat varieties – in boiling water some can soften in less than a minute – so to avoid soggy results, soaking is safer. Choose hot or cold water depending on the rest of the recipe and how quickly you'll need the noodles – freshly soaked is best to prevent the risk of them sticking before you're ready to dress, or to add to your soup, curry or stir-fry. Rice vermicelli will take 25–30 minutes to soften in cold water, 5–7 minutes in freshly boiled water. Wider flat rice noodles, like those found in pad thai, can take from 20 to 30 minutes to soften in hot water.

Starchy noodles like glass (cellophane) require very little soaking – just 5–10 minutes for some in hot water – but as the different varieties are made from different ingredients, follow the advice on the packet. Soba noodles are the starchiest of the wheat varieties and therefore require slightly different handling to avoid ending up with a sticky, solid lump that won't separate into individual strands. After boiling or soaking, submerge the noodles in a big bowl of cold water. Swish about with your hands to rinse off most of the starch, then leave in a colander or sieve to drain thoroughly. If they're being used in a hot dish, rather than a salad, submerging back into hot water is the easiest way to reheat. It's also worth briefly rinsing glass noodles before adding to dishes, but this can be more simply done in a sieve under running water.

If in doubt, following the packet instructions is a good starting point, but always bear in mind where the noodles will end up.

For broths and soups: thinner noodles will continue to soften as they hang around in the broth, so it's important not to overcook them to start with. If using dried glass noodles, simply add straight to the soup – no soaking required.

For stir-fries: don't soften noodles too thoroughly as they'll cook a little more in the pan and sauce.

For salads: cook or soak until totally ready to eat, then rinse under cold water to cool quickly. Drying on kitchen paper is a good way to avoid watery salads and diluting the flavour of your dressings.

HOW TO SERVE

Whether you're a chopstick fan or favour a good old fork, most dishes are best served straight away as those sauce-sucking noodles can turn a little claggy if left sitting around for ages. Batching salads works, as cooked noodles keep in the fridge for a few days, but you might just want to hold back some dressing so you can refresh each day.

Surplus stir-fry can be revived with a splash more water, soy sauce or similar, to add sauciness when reheating – but to avoid overcooking, it's best done in the microwave second time around. The same goes for frozen leftovers – the freezer isn't really noodle-friendly, as the noodles can quickly dry out and break up on reheating, but if you don't mind broken noodles or adding a little extra sauce, they're best frozen for short periods of no more than a month.

As you'll know from eating in Chinese and Thai restaurants, extra condiments on the table are a must. Dark soy sauce, chilli oils and chilli sauces all add extra depth to dishes, whereas Japanese tables may offer pickles as garnishes. And a good squeeze of lemon or lime is great for adding freshness to a curry.

For Instagram-worthy noodle twirls, soak sticks of noodles in a shallow tray or dish instead of a bowl – this will keep the strands neatly lined up. Lift out small bunches to drain on kitchen paper, then wind around a spare chopstick for that tightly coiled, spiral finish. Snap away.

ESSENTIAL STORE-CUPBOARD KIT

It's good to have a well-stocked store cupboard for all your non-perishables – including dried noodles – and particularly useful for the more unusual ingredients you might use less regularly. Oils, sauces, spices, seeds, stock, nuts and pastes are a few essentials for pimping noodles – just check after opening if they need to be kept in the fridge.

Coconut milk and cream: great for vegans, great for curries!

Crispy fried onions: add texture and flavour – store-bought or make your own (see page 15).

Curry pastes: keep a range. A little goes a long way with Thai red, green and yellow. Indonesian rendang is more unusual, but supermarkets usually stock a wide variety of Indian pastes.

Fish sauce: adds saltiness to Thai and Vietnamese noodles.

Flavourless oils: good for stir-frying – vegetable, sunflower, groundnut and light rapeseed all work well.

Honey and maple syrup: maple is good for vegans, and both are reasonably interchangeable if used in small amounts.

Kecap manis: Indonesian sweet soy sauce.

Light and dark soy sauce: lighter is saltier, and the soy sauce go-to if the recipe doesn't prescribe, but dark is richer and adds colour to marinades and sauces. For a gluten-free option, substitute with tamari (a naturally gluten-free alternative to soy sauce).

Miso pastes: made from fermented soy beans; white is the sweetest, brown and red are usually saltier.

Nut butters: use for satay-style flavours and adding protein to vegan and veggie dishes.

Rice vinegar: mild, Asian vinegar.

Sesame oil: look for richer, toasted varieties.

Spices: this book mainly uses the Asian spice shelf, so keep things like curry powders, ground turmeric and Chinese five-spice in stock.

Sriracha: Thai hot sauce made from chilli paste.

Stock powders and pots: in clear soups and broths it can be worth using a stock pot over a cube. If following a gluten-free diet, make sure to use a wheat-free brand.

Sweet and sweet-hot chilli sauces: choose your favourite brands.

Tahini: like a sesame version of peanut butter; good for making creamy salad dressings without adding dairy.

A NOTE ON THE RECIPES

All of the following recipes include labels that let you know when the dish is dairy, gluten or egg free (along with vegetarian or vegan). If you follow one of these diets, please ensure that you use the version of the above store-cupboard ingredients that best suits your dietary requirements.

It's also worth noting that whenever a recipe includes an instruction to season, this means salt and freshly ground pepper, unless otherwise stated. Similarly, if a recipe calls for oil, feel free to use any flavourless oil you have spare in your cupboard (sunflower, vegetable or rapeseed, for example). If a specific oil is needed, it will be specified in the ingredients list (such as sesame).

OVEN TEMPERATURE GUIDE

	ELEC °C	ELEC °F	ELEC °C (FAN)	GAS MARK
COOL	140	275	120	1
MODERATE	160	325	140	3
MODERATELY HOT	200	400	180	6
HOT	220	425	200	7

WEIGHT MEASUREMENTS

METRIC	IMPERIAL
10G	½ OZ
20G	¾ OZ
25G	1 OZ
50G	2 OZ
75G	3 OZ
125G	4½ OZ
150G	5 OZ
200G	7 OZ
250G	9 OZ
350G	12 OZ
450G	1LB

LIQUID MEASUREMENTS

METRIC	IMPERIAL	AUSTRALIAN/US
25ML	1FL OZ	
60ML	2 FL OZ	¼ CUP
100ML	3½ FL OZ	
120ML	4 FL OZ	½ CUP
150ML	5 FL OZ	
200ML	7 FL OZ	
250ML	9 FL OZ	1 CUP
400ML	14 FL OZ	1¾ CUPS
450ML	16 FL OZ	2 CUPS
600ML	1 PINT	2½ CUPS
750ML	1¼ PINTS	3 CUPS
900ML	1½ PINTS	3½ CUPS
1 LITRE	1¾ PINTS	1 QUART OR 4 CUPS
1.2 LITRES	2 PINTS	
2 LITRES	3½ PINTS	

FIVE FAST SALAD DRESSINGS

A good dressing can turn any old noodles into a flavour-packed salad.
Just add some veg and protein to complete the dish.

GINGER-MISO DRESSING

Makes Enough For 2 Servings
Takes Less Than 5 Minutes

Whisk 1 tbsp white miso paste with 2 tbsp rice vinegar and 1 tbsp sesame oil. Grate in a ball of stem ginger and season.

SOUTH-EAST ASIAN SWEET & SOUR DRESSING

Makes Enough For 4 Servings
Takes Less Than 5 Minutes

Whisk together 3 tbsp lime juice, 2 tbsp fish sauce and 3 tbsp water.

For Vietnamese nuoc-cham-style dressing, add 2 tbsp caster sugar and 1–2 diced fresh red chillies.

For a spicy Thai version, gently crush 2–3 small dried red chillies with 1½ tbsp palm sugar in a pestle and mortar, then mix with the rest of the dressing.

STICKY SOY DRESSING

Makes Enough For 4 Servings
Takes Less Than 5 Minutes

Mix together 3 tbsp kecap manis, 2 tbsp dark soy sauce, ½ tsp freshly grated ginger and 1 tbsp rice vinegar or lime juice.

NUT BUTTER SATAY DRESSING

Makes Enough For 3–4 Servings
Takes Less Than 5 Minutes

Whizz in a blender or mini food processor 50g smooth nut butter, 2 tsp light soy sauce, 2 tsp maple syrup, ½ teaspoon freshly grated ginger or purée, the juice from ½ lime and 2 tbsp water. Season with the juice from the remaining ½ lime, until tasty.

GREEN CHILLI & HERB DRESSING

Makes Enough For 3–4 Servings
Takes Less Than 5 Minutes

Put 1 green chilli (deseeded or not depending on how spicy you like it), 2 tbsp flavourless oil (see store-cupboard essentials, page 10), 1 tsp fish sauce, 1 tsp caster sugar, a handful each of mint and coriander leaves and the zest and juice of 1 lime into a mini food processor. Pulse to make
a pesto-like dressing and then season with some salt before using quickly – it's best freshly made!

FIVE TASTY TOPPINGS

Pimping your noodles with your favourite condiments is just the start. Soft, chewy, slurpy noodles are crying out for a crunchy, crispy, oozy topping like toasted nuts, coconut shavings, chopped spring onions or one of these minimal-effort ideas to keep things even more interesting.

SHORTCUT PICKLED VEG

Makes enough for 2–4 servings
Takes 10 minutes + marinating
Mix 3 tbsp rice vinegar and 4 tsp caster sugar with 1 tsp sesame seeds (any colour). When the sugar has dissolved, stir in 2 thinly sliced shallots, 4 thinly sliced radishes and 1 carrot, peeled into ribbons. Stir occasionally for 30 minutes until the veg is still crisp, but nicely pickled.

JAMMY EGGS

Makes as many as you want
Takes 20 minutes
Fill a large saucepan with water to a depth of about 10cm and bring to the boil. Add large, room-temperature eggs, reduce the heat to a simmer and cook for 7 minutes before plunging the eggs quickly into very cold water. Peel after 10 minutes.

TONKATSU SAUCE

Makes enough for 2–4 servings
Takes less than 5 minutes

Mix 5 tbsp tomato ketchup, 3 tbsp Worcestershire sauce, 1 tsp honey and 2 tsp dark soy sauce. Drizzle over Japanese noodles, or use as a dip.

HOMEMADE CRISPY FRIED ONIONS

Make as many as you want
Takes 20 minutes

Thinly slice peeled shallots on a mandolin. Fill a wok with sunflower oil to a depth of about 4cm, then heat until the surface shimmers and shallot slices start bubbling instantly when dropped in carefully. Fry in small batches until golden brown and crisp then remove with a slotted spoon and drain on kitchen paper. Keep in an airtight container for 2 weeks.

FURIKAKE SEASONING

Makes 16 servings
Takes 10 minutes

Toast 50g mixed sesame seeds until fragrant, then tip into a bowl with 1 tsp sea salt and cool. Use kitchen scissors to first snip 2 nori sheets into fine strips, then stack the strips and cut the other way into tiny squares, so they fall into the sesame seeds. Stir in with ½ tsp caster sugar. Non-vegetarian option: use the scissors to also snip in 1 tbsp bonito flakes (dried flakes of tuna you'll find in Asian stores).

Super Easy
10-Minute Fixes

LEMON, PARMESAN & PISTACHIO

MARMITE BUTTER & BACON

MISO-MUSHROOM & HERB

FRENCH ONION PHO

SHAKEN-JAR SRIRACHA SAUCE

SINGAPORE SCRAMBLE

NOODLE OMELETTE ROLL-UPS

SWEET SOY SALMON

BUTTERED GOCHUJANG

AVO-TOPPED TAHINI

LEMON, PARMESAN & PISTACHIO

VEGETARIAN OPTION:

replace the Parmesan with a vegetarian hard cheese

Ingredients

1 nest of medium egg noodles

1 tbsp salted butter

2 tbsp chopped pistachios

zest and juice of ½ lemon

handful of finely grated or shaved Parmesan

handful of spinach leaves

Serves 1
Takes less than 10 minutes

Cook the noodles following the packet instructions and reserve a ladleful of the cooking liquid before draining. Put the butter, pistachios, lemon zest and juice into a saucepan with 2 tablespoons of the cooking water. Turn up the heat while whisking together until the butter is melted and the sauce is bubbling. Grind in plenty of black pepper, then toss in the noodles. Take off the heat and mix through the cheese and spinach leaves. If the noodles look a little dry, add a splash more of the noodle cooking water.

NOODLE SWAP: try any wholewheat noodles cooked according to the packet instructions.

MARMITE BUTTER & BACON

Ingredients

2 rashers unsmoked back or streaky bacon, diced

2 tsp Marmite

1 tbsp room-temperature butter

1 x 150g sachet straight-to-wok thick egg noodles

only if there is one already in your fridge – a chopped spring onion

Serves 1
Takes 10 minutes

Fry the bacon in a splash of oil in a frying pan until crispy. Meanwhile, mash the Marmite with the butter and some salt and pepper. Toss the noodles into the pan to coat in the bacon bits and oil, then stir through the butter until all the noodle strands are well coated. Add a splash of water if the noodles are looking dry, and eat with a scattering of chopped spring onion, if using.

NOODLE SWAP:
thick udon noodles give even more comfort factor.

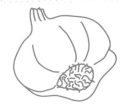

MISO-MUSHROOM & HERB

VEGAN

Ingredients

50g dried wholegrain or white vermicelli noodles

75g mushrooms of choice, or a mixture, sliced

2 garlic cloves, crushed

1 tbsp miso paste (any colour)

2 tsp sesame oil

small handful of mixed coriander leaves and snipped chives

**Serves 1
Takes 10 minutes**

While you soak the noodles in boiling water until just soft, fry the mushrooms and garlic in a splash of oil until softened and starting to brown. Push the mushrooms to the side of the pan and mash the miso paste and sesame oil with a glug of the noodle soaking liquid to loosen the sauce. Tip the drained, softened noodles into the pan with the mushrooms and toss everything together to combine. Take off the heat and toss through the herbs.

NOODLE SWAP:
fine egg noodles.

FRENCH ONION PHO

VEGETARIAN + GLUTEN FREE
(but check the soup brand)

Ingredients

25g dried flat rice noodles

1 x 400g tin French onion soup

1 star anise

2 tsp light soy sauce or tamari

a few coriander leaves

a few Homemade crispy fried onions (see page 15) or ready-made, to serve (optional)

**Serves 1
Takes less than 10 minutes**

Put the noodles into the bottom of a small, lidded saucepan, then pour the soup over the top so they are submerged. Add the star anise and soy sauce, cover, and bring to the boil over a high heat. Simmer for 2–3 minutes until the noodles are tender but still retain a little bite, then fish out the star anise as you pour everything into a wide bowl to eat. Scatter with the coriander and a few crispy onions if you fancy.

NOODLE SWAP: you can use straight-to-wok rice noodles too; just warm through to serve and simmer the soup for a couple of minutes with the star anise first.

SHAKEN-JAR SRIRACHA SAUCE

`VEGETARIAN + DAIRY FREE`

Ingredients

1 tbsp soy sauce

1 tbsp crunchy peanut butter

1 tbsp sriracha chilli sauce

1 tsp runny honey

2 tbsp boiling water

1 x 150g sachet straight-to-wok noodles
– choose your favourite

**Serves 1
Takes less than 5 minutes**

Put everything except the noodles into a glass jar, screw on the lid and shake vigorously until you have a smooth sauce. Tip into a pan with the noodles and stir-fry for 2 minutes until the noodles are coated in the sticky sauce.

NOODLE SWAP: try udon or, for gluten free, flat rice noodles and tamari.

SINGAPORE SCRAMBLE

`VEGETARIAN + GLUTEN FREE`

Ingredients

2 eggs

1 tsp mild curry powder

small knob of butter

2 spring onions, finely sliced

150g cooked Singapore rice noodles
– use straight-to-wok sachets or
find bags of fresh near the stir-fry
vegetable packets in supermarkets

lemon juice, to serve

**Serves 1
Takes 5 minutes**

Whisk the eggs into the curry powder one by one, with plenty of seasoning. Over a gentle heat, melt the butter in a frying pan, then tip in the eggs and scramble for a minute or two. While still a little soft, toss in the spring onions and noodles. Stir-fry together for 2 minutes, then eat – with a splash of lemon juice.

NOODLE SWAP: plain rice vermicelli noodles with an extra teaspoon of curry powder.

NOODLE OMELETTE ROLL-UPS

DAIRY FREE + GLUTEN FREE + VEGETARIAN
(depending on choice of filling)

Serves 1
Takes 5 minutes

Ingredients

small handful of coriander leaves

2 large eggs, beaten with a fork

1 tsp light soy sauce or tamari

handful of soaked or fresh rice
    vermicelli noodles

your choice: small handful of shredded
    cooked chicken, cooked prawns or
    black beans

sweet or hot chilli sauce

Finely chop a few of the coriander leaves and mix into the eggs with the soy
sauce. Brush a medium-sized non-stick frying pan with a little oil, then swirl
in the egg mixture to coat the base. Cook for a few minutes, using a small
spatula to keep releasing the egg around the edges, until the top is set. In
the pan – or you can carefully slide the omelette out onto a board or plate –
spread the noodles across the middle of the omelette in a strip. Top with the
rest of the coriander leaves followed by your choice of chicken, prawns or
beans. Squirt over your favourite chilli sauce, then gently roll up and eat.

NOODLE SWAP: fine noodles work best – try thin egg or
glass noodles instead.

SWEET SOY SALMON

DAIRY FREE

Serves 1
Takes 5 minutes

Ingredients

3 tbsp kecap manis

1 tbsp lime juice

¼ tsp freshly grated ginger or ginger purée

1 x 150g sachet straight-to-wok medium egg noodles

1 small, cooked salmon fillet

small handful of coriander or rocket leaves

Tip the kecap manis, lime juice and ginger into a pan with a splash of oil and keep stirring until hot. Cook the noodles in a separate pan with a little oil for 2 minutes. When warm, place on a plate and flake the salmon in decent chunks, discarding the skin, on top. Pour over the sauce and finally, add the coriander or rocket and eat.

NOODLE SWAP: you can try almost any in this versatile sauce, and it's also good cold the next day for lunch.

BUTTERED GOCHUJANG

VEGETARIAN + EGG FREE

Ingredients

1 x 150g sachet straight-to-wok udon
 noodles

2–3 tbsp kimchee, roughly chopped

1 tbsp butter

1 tbsp gochujang Korean chilli paste

2 tsp runny honey

Serves 1
Takes less than 10 minutes

Microwave the noodles following the packet instructions – straight-to-wok udon noodles are much easier to stir-fry if they're already hot and loosening. If you don't have a microwave, running a kettle of boiling water over them in a sieve will also help them ease apart. Stir-fry the rest of the ingredients together until the sauce is sizzling, then toss through the noodles.

NOODLE SWAP:
thick noodles work best with this chunky sauce.

AVO-TOPPED TAHINI

VEGAN + DAIRY AND EGG FREE + GLUTEN FREE
if using rice noodles

Ingredients

75g brown rice flat noodles or wholewheat noodles

1 tbsp tahini

1 tsp light soy sauce or tamari

juice of ½ small lemon (keep the other half)

1 tsp toasted or black sesame seeds

1 small, ripe avocado, diced

Serves 1
Takes 10 minutes

Soak the noodles in boiling water following the packet timings, until just tender, then drain. Meanwhile, mash the tahini in a decent-sized bowl to loosen, before mashing in the soy sauce and lemon juice. Work in 1 tbsp water until you have a smooth but thick sauce, then stir in some of the sesame seeds. Tip the drained noodles into the bowl, using your hands to coat them all in the dressing. Scatter with the avocado chunks, sprinkle with the remaining seeds and some black pepper, and then add a squeeze more lemon juice if you think it needs it.

NOODLE SWAP: if you're not worried about gluten, try soba or another buckwheat noodle instead.

FRESH SALADS

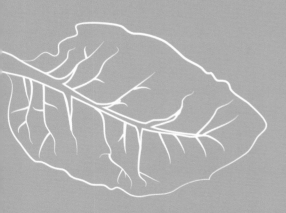

SATAY CHICKEN NOODLE

SUPER-GREEN NOODLE WITH TAHINI DRESSING

THAI SOM TAM WITH SWEDE & GLASS NOODLES

CHINESE SHREDDED DUCK, CLEMENTINE & NOODLE

SHREDDED CABBAGE, APPLE & MISO SLAW

PORK PATTIES WITH VIETNAMESE NOODLE

GREEN MANGO & RICE NOODLE WITH CRAB

CRUNCHY VEG GOODNESS BOWL WITH EGGS

ROAST SWEET POTATO & SALMON NOODLE

THAI-STYLE WATERMELON, GREEN BEAN & CASHEW

SATAY CHICKEN NOODLE SALAD

GLUTEN FREE + DAIRY AND EGG FREE

Ingredients

200g dried flat rice noodles

1 tbsp toasted sesame oil

2 quantities Nut butter satay dressing (see page 13 – make with peanut butter)

150–175g hunk of green, white or savoy cabbage, shredded

2 large carrots, cut into matchsticks

small bunch of mint, leaves picked and large ones torn

350g cooked chicken, shredded

25g roasted peanuts, roughly chopped

For the quick pickled shallots

2 long or 4 round shallots, finely sliced

2 tbsp rice vinegar

1 tsp caster or granulated sugar

To serve

1 lime, cut into wedges

For a classic satay flavour, make the nut butter dressing for this with a smooth peanut variety – extra nuts at the end add crunch.

Serves 4 for dinner, 6 for a lunch
Takes less than 30 minutes

Soak the noodles in a big bowl of hot water for about 20 minutes until soft. Rinse with cold water then drain and pat dry before tossing with the sesame oil in a big bowl.

Mix the shallots with the vinegar and sugar and set aside to pickle, stirring occasionally – they'll turn pale pink when they're ready.

Pour half the satay dressing over the noodles and mix through to coat every strand. Add the cabbage, carrots and most of the mint leaves and toss a few more times to distribute the vegetables evenly.

Divide the salad between serving plates, top with the shredded chicken and drizzle generously with some more dressing. Scatter with the reserved mint, pickled shallots and chopped peanuts. Serve with lime wedges.

NOODLE SWAP: save soaking time with straight-to-wok rice noodles. Microwaving first will help them absorb the dressing, but don't add the mint until they've cooled down.

SUPER-GREEN NOODLE SALAD WITH TAHINI DRESSING

VEGETARIAN

Ingredients

100g dried brown flat rice noodles

150g frozen edamame beans

12cm piece of cucumber, chunkily diced

75g sugar snap peas, sliced

big handful of coriander, roughly chopped

2 tsp mixed seeds

For the dressing

50g tahini

2 tsp light soy sauce

3 tbsp cider vinegar

2 tsp honey (or maple syrup if vegan)

Swap the seed mix for furikake, if you've got some, to add a Japanese twist to this super-healthy salad.

Serves 2
Takes less than 25 minutes

Soak the noodles in hot water until tender, then rinse under cold water and drain well. Blanch the edamame beans for a minute in boiling water then refresh under cold water to cool and drain.

Whisk together the dressing ingredients with 1 tbsp water in a big mixing bowl. Season with salt and pepper. Tip the noodles, edamame, cucumber, sugar snap peas and coriander on top and toss to coat everything thoroughly. Scatter with the seeds to serve.

> **NOODLE SWAP:**
> chewy soba noodles are also a great match for this dressing.

THAI SOM TAM SALAD WITH SWEDE & GLASS NOODLES

VEGAN
Just use the Green chilli & herb dressing instead
(see page 13)

Ingredients

**75g green beans, trimmed and
quartered**

50g dried glass noodles

**½ quantity (4–5 tbsp) South-east
Asian sweet & sour dressing (see
page 12 – make the Thai version)**

6 cherry tomatoes, halved

1 tsp tamarind paste, finely shredded

300g hunk of swede

**2 tbsp roasted peanuts, roughly
chopped**

handful of coriander leaves

*This twist on the Thai classic uses swede in place
of green papaya. Once finely shredded, raw swede
has a crisp texture and peppery finish similar to
radish but softens after soaking in the dressing.
Dried shrimp makes an authentic, but optional,
topping for non-vegetarians/vegans.*

Serves 2
Takes less than 20 minutes

Blanch the green beans for a minute in boiling water, then
drain and rinse under cold water to cool quickly. Soak the
glass noodles until tender, then rinse and drain well.

Put the dressing in a big mixing bowl with the tomatoes
and tamarind paste. Squish the tomatoes with a fork, mixing
the juices and tamarind into the dressing as you do so.
Shred the swede with a julienne peeler – or matchstick
as finely as you can. Add the swede to the bowl along
with the beans, noodles, peanuts and coriander leaves.
Season with salt and pepper, toss well and serve.

> **NOODLE SWAP:**
> rice vermicelli.

CHINESE SHREDDED DUCK, CLEMENTINE & NOODLE SALAD

DAIRY FREE

Ingredients

2 confit duck legs, or ½ aromatic crispy duck

1 x 300g tin mandarin or clementine segments

100ml hoisin sauce

2 tbsp rice vinegar

350g fresh straight-to-wok egg noodles, cooked following the packet instructions then cooled and drained

50g soft salad leaves – pea shoots, lamb's lettuce, spinach, or a mixture

½ cucumber, deseeded and sliced into half-moons

sharing bag of prawn crackers

Supermarket cheats never tasted so good – and this warm salad uses every trick in the book to make this the easiest fakeaway ever.

Serves 4
Takes less than 40 minutes depending on the duck – but only 10 minutes of effort

Cook the duck following the packet instructions. Meanwhile, make a salad dressing. Drain the tinned fruit over a bowl to catch the juices. Put a tablespoon of the juice into a jug with the hoisin sauce and rice vinegar. Season with some black pepper and whisk together. Stir the dressing through the noodles.

When the duck is cool enough to handle, shred the meat from the bones in bite-size chunks. You can discard the skin, or shred the crispy bits to use in the salad too.

Use your biggest platter to build the dish, layering the dressed noodles and handfuls of leaves with the duck meat, citrus segments and cucumber. Crunch a couple of handfuls of prawn crackers over the top, and serve the rest on the side.

NOODLE SWAP: use long-life packets of straight-to-wok egg noodles from the store cupboard, cooked, cooled and drained.

SHREDDED CABBAGE, APPLE & MISO SLAW

VEGAN

Ingredients

100g dried flat rice noodles or black noodles

2 green apples, quartered and cored

4 small round shallots, thinly sliced

250g hunk of savoy cabbage, woody core cut away

1 tbsp poppy seeds

1 quantity Ginger-miso dressing (see page 12)

If you like things spicy, add some sliced green chillies to this fresh salad – even spicier, keep the seeds in!

Serves 4
Takes 15 minutes

Soak the noodles in hot water until tender, then sieve, rinse well with cold water and dry on kitchen paper.

Slice the apples as thinly as you can. Put the apple and shallots in a big mixing bowl. Finely shred the cabbage and add to the bowl with the noodles and poppy seeds. Pour over the dressing and toss everything together.

NOODLE SWAP:
try thin rice vermicelli noodles.

PORK PATTIES WITH VIETNAMESE NOODLE SALAD

EGG AND DAIRY FREE + GLUTEN FREE

Make sure your sausages are gluten-free

Ingredients

4 small round shallots

1 lemongrass stalk

1 garlic clove

250g pork mince

250g pork sausages, meat squeezed from the skins

1 tsp fish sauce

1 quantity Green chilli & herb dressing (see page 13)

150g dried rice vermicelli noodles

2 courgettes, peeled into ribbons, or 1 x 300g bag of spiralised courgetti

small bunch of mint, leaves picked

The punchy green chilli and herb dressing is quick to add flavour to any number of things, so here it's used twice – as the noodle dressing, but also to flavour the pork patties.

Serves 4
Takes less than 40 minutes

Very finely chop 2 of the shallots, the lemongrass stalk and garlic – or put them in a mini food processor and pulse to chop together. Fry in a splash of oil for a few minutes until aromatic. Cool for 5 minutes, then tip into a mixing bowl with the pork mince, sausage meat, fish sauce and 2 tablespoons of the dressing. Season with salt and pepper, then use your hands to squish together well and shape into about 16 patties. Chill for 10 minutes.

Soak the noodles until tender, then rinse well in cold water before draining and drying with kitchen paper. Tip into another mixing bowl with the rest of the dressing, the courgette and most of the mint leaves. Dice the remaining shallots, add to the salad and toss together.

Heat a tablespoon of oil in a large frying pan and cook the pork patties in two batches for 4–5 minutes on each side until golden and cooked through. Or brush with oil and bake at 200°C/180°C fan/gas 6 for 10–12 minutes.

Serve the patties on top of the salad, with the remaining mint leaves scattered over the top.

NOODLE SWAP:
flat rice noodles.

GREEN MANGO & RICE NOODLE SALAD WITH CRAB

GLUTEN FREE + DAIRY AND EGG FREE

Ingredients

- 200g straight-to-wok rice vermicelli noodles, cooked following the packet instructions then cooled
- ½ quantity (4–5 tbsp) South-east Asian sweet & sour dressing (see page 12 – make the Vietnamese version)
- ½ large, ripe mango, peeled and thinly sliced into half-moons
- 2 spring onions, thinly sliced on the diagonal
- small handful of mint leaves
- small handful of Thai basil leaves
- small handful of coriander leaves
- 100g white crab meat, fresh or tinned (drained)

Crab might be a treat, but a little goes a long way in this full-flavoured salad – with sweet mango balancing sharply dressed noodles.

Serves 2
Takes less than 15 minutes

Tip the noodles into a mixing bowl with the sweet sour dressing. Toss to coat a few times. Add the mango, most of the spring onion, all of the herbs and a tablespoon of the crab meat. Toss very gently to work all of the ingredients through the noodles.

Divide the noodles between bowls or plates then top with the rest of the crab meat and scatter with the remaining spring onion.

> **NOODLE SWAP:** glass or black rice noodles.

CRUNCHY VEG GOODNESS BOWL WITH EGGS

VEGETARIAN

Ingredients

75–85g dried soba noodles

125g thin-stemmed broccoli, trimmed

handful of kale leaves, thick stalks discarded

125g hunk of red cabbage, very finely sliced

1 small, ripe avocado, sliced

2 Jammy eggs (see page 14), halved

2 tsp pumpkin seeds

For the dressing

50g tahini

1½ lemons

1 very small garlic clove, crushed

¼–½ tsp honey

Once you've made your dressed noodles and jammy eggs, the rest is really up to you. Blanched greens, roasted roots, whatever you've got in the fridge that looks like it needs using up!

Serves 2
Takes 30 minutes

Soak the noodles in cold water until soft. Rinse the starch off thoroughly then drain well.

Make the dressing by mashing the tahini with the zest of ½ lemon, the juice of 1 lemon and the garlic. Stir in 2 tbsp water to a smooth, runny consistency and season. Add ¼ teaspoon of honey to begin with – taste and if it needs more sweetness add another ¼ teaspoon.

Bring half a saucepan of water to the boil. Add the broccoli spears and blanch for 2 minutes, then take off the heat and, working quickly, submerge the kale in the water before draining everything immediately.

Toss the noodles with half the dressing, then arrange on two plates with the broccoli, kale and red cabbage. Add the avocado with the remaining lemon half squeezed over. Drizzle the rest of the dressing over everything, top with freshly halved jammy eggs and scatter with the pumpkin seeds.

> **NOODLE SWAP:**
> other wholewheat noodle varieties.

ROAST SWEET POTATO & SALMON NOODLE SALAD

`DAIRY AND EGG FREE`

Ingredients

2 small sweet potatoes (about 175g each), peeled if you like and cut into bite-size chunks

1½ tbsp extra virgin olive or rapeseed oil

2 small or 1 large salmon fillet

½ quantity Sticky soy dressing (see page 13)

3 spring onions, finely sliced

85g dried soba noodles, soaked to soften, rinsed and drained

2 big handfuls of baby salad leaves

For variation, try swapping the salmon with no-need-to-cook hot smoked mackerel – sustainable and flavour-packed. A double batch means effortless packed lunches the following day.

Serves 2
Takes 30 minutes

Preheat the oven to 200°C/180°C fan/gas 6 and toss the potato chunks with 1 tablespoon of the oil on a roasting tray. Season and roast for 15 minutes. Flip the potatoes and move to make space to add the salmon to the tray, skin-side down. Brush the top of the salmon with a little of the sticky soy dressing, then bake for 10–12 minutes to cook the fish through. If the potatoes aren't soft yet, just lift out the fish and put them back in the oven for a couple more minutes.

Tip the potatoes into a big bowl with most of the spring onion and the noodles. Drizzle over the rest of the oil followed by the soy dressing, and toss to combine. Flake over the fish, discarding the skin, and toss gently just once or twice more so it doesn't disintegrate. Scatter with the remaining spring onion slices to serve – on a bed of leaves.

> **NOODLE SWAP:** any wholewheat or brown rice options make for a meal with added benefits.

THAI-STYLE WATERMELON, GREEN BEAN & CASHEW SALAD

VEGAN

Ingredients

150g dried flat rice noodles

200g green beans. trimmed

300g hunk of watermelon, flesh cut into small wedges

small bunch of mint, leaves picked

3 tbsp lime juice

75g roasted and salted cashew nuts

1 quantity Nut butter satay dressing (see page 13 – made with cashew butter)

2 tbsp Homemade crispy fried onions (see page 15) or ready-made

This modern, colourful salad makes a great vegan main course, but also a brilliant side to serve at a sunny barbecue. If taking to a friend's house or to work for lunch, simply carry the salad, mint, dressing and fried shallots separately, and combine everything before serving.

Serves 4 (or 8 as a side)
Takes 20 minutes

Soak the noodles in a big bowl of hot water for 20 minutes until soft. Meanwhile, blanch the green beans in boiling for 3–4 minutes, then refresh in cold water to cool them quickly and dry on kitchen paper. Refresh and dry the noodles in the same way.

Gently toss the noodles, beans, watermelon wedges and mint leaves with the lime juice. Add most of the cashews, breaking them up in your hands a little as you do so, and mix a couple more times. Tip the salad onto a serving dish and drizzle over the satay dressing. Scatter with the remaining cashews and the crispy onions.

> **NOODLE SWAP:**
> try rice vermicelli noodles.

Sizzling Stir Fries

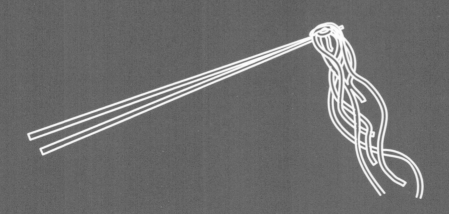

CROWD-PLEASING PAD THAI

KIMCHEE FRIED NOODLES

DAN DAN-DON'T NOODLES

FIRECRACKER PRAWN NOODLES

DUCK & HOISIN CHOW MEIN

CRISPY FRIED NOODLES WITH CHICKEN,
CHILLIES AND HOLY BASIL

CHINESE CHILLI BEEF & BLACK BEAN PAN-FRY

SWEET & SOUR AUBERGINES

EGG-FRIED NOODLES WITH CHAR SIU PORK

MISO FRIED GREENS WITH UDON NOODLES

CROWD-PLEASING PAD THAI

VEGAN + GLUTEN FREE

(depending on choice of toppings)

Ingredients

225g dried flat rice noodles

1 quantity Nut butter satay dressing (see page 13)

1 tbsp tamarind paste (or 1 tsp concentrated)

200g firm tofu

1 tbsp sesame oil

200g beansprouts

75g roasted peanuts, roughly chopped

6 spring onions, finely sliced

To serve

roughly chopped coriander, Jammy eggs (see page 14), shredded chicken, lime wedges, fish sauce and soy sauce

A great stir-fry to enjoy with mates — whatever their dietary dos and don'ts. The main recipe is vegan, then you can mix up the toppings to suit yourself.

Serves 3–4
Takes less than 20 minutes

Soak the noodles in hot water for 20 minutes until soft. Rinse with cold water and drain. Mix together the satay dressing and tamarind paste to make a sauce. Crumble the tofu finely with your fingers until it looks a bit like cooked mince.

Heat the sesame oil and 1 tbsp flavourless oil in a large wok. Add the crumbled tofu and fry for 3 minutes — scrape up any crispy bits sticking to the pan. Tip in the drained noodles, beansprouts, most of the peanuts and half the spring onions and stir-fry for 2 minutes. Pour over the sauce and toss well to coat all the ingredients evenly. Once everything is heated through, season with salt and serve scattered with the rest of the peanuts and spring onions.

Put the coriander, jammy eggs and chicken in separate bowls for people to help themselves, and serve along with a pile of lime wedges and some fish and soy sauce for extra seasoning.

NOODLE SWAP: stick to the classic unless you fancy a brown rice version.

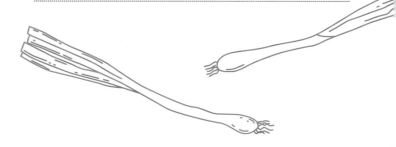

KIMCHEE FRIED NOODLES

VEGAN

Ingredients

85g dried wholewheat noodles
1 red or white onion, sliced
2 garlic cloves, sliced
1 large carrot, cut into matchsticks
**1 large red or yellow pepper, deseeded
and thinly sliced**
125g Chinese leaf, shredded
100g kimchee
1 tsp sesame oil
2 tsp sesame seeds
2 spring onions, thinly sliced

*If you're feeling run down, forget the chicken soup –
these veg-packed noodles not only deliver a vitamin
boost, but a good hit of gut-friendly bacteria from
the Korean kimchee. Superfood in a stir-fry.*

Serves 2
Takes less than 15 minutes

Boil the noodles until tender, then drain.

Meanwhile, heat 2 tsp oil in a wok or frying pan. Fry the onion
for 1 minute, then add the garlic, carrot and pepper and fry for
2 minutes. Add the Chinese leaf and stir-fry for 1 more minute.

Add the noodles to the pan with the kimchee and sesame oil.
Stir-fry briefly until everything is piping hot. Toss through the
sesame seeds and spring onions and serve.

> **NOODLE SWAP:**
> flat brown rice noodles.

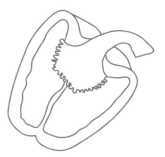

DAN DAN-DON'T NOODLES

VEGAN

Ingredients

300g chestnut or other mushrooms, diced

½ tsp Chinese five-spice powder

300g straight-to-wok udon noodles

3 spring onions, finely sliced

1 tbsp finely chopped roasted peanuts

For the sauce

2 tbsp smooth peanut butter

1 tbsp light soy sauce

1 tbsp Chinkiang (black) vinegar or balsamic

1 tbsp Chinese chilli oil, plus extra to serve (optional)

⅛ tsp ground Sichuan peppercorns

This is a fun veggie version of the Sichuan classic, where you don't need minced meat. Use proper Chinese chilli oil – it's thick with dried, crushed chillies, not just a flavoured oil.

Serves 2
Takes less than 30 minutes

Put the sauce ingredients in a small saucepan with 2 tbsp water and whisk as it heats through. When the sauce is smooth, take the pan off the heat.

Heat 1 tbsp oil in a large wok. Stir-fry the mushrooms over a high heat until all the moisture has evaporated and they've turned brown and are starting to crisp around the edges. Stir in the Chinese five-spice powder and fry for another 30–60 seconds until the mushrooms are really becoming crispy. Add the noodles and, using tongs, heat them while tossing with the mushrooms. Take the pan off the heat and add the sauce with the spring onions and peanuts and keep tossing for another minute to mix everything thoroughly. Eat with extra chilli oil if you dare.

NOODLE SWAP: use a thick wheat noodle for sauce-sucking properties.

FIRECRACKER PRAWN NOODLES

DAIRY AND EGG FREE + GLUTEN FREE

check the cornflour label and use rice noodles for a gluten-free option

Ingredients

75g dried flat wheat noodles

150–200g peeled king prawns

1 tsp cornflour

3–4 tsp sriracha (depending on how spicy you like it!)

2 tbsp tomato ketchup

2 tbsp sweet chilli sauce

1 onion, peeled and cut into thin wedges

2 small red, yellow or orange peppers (or a mixture), cut into big bite-size chunks

1 x 225g tin water chestnuts, drained

2 fat garlic cloves, thinly sliced

2 tsp ginger purée or freshly grated ginger

2 spring onions, thinly sliced

If you keep a bag of prawns in your freezer, this simple stir-fry basically turns into a store-cupboard supper – great for those last-minute dinner dilemmas.

Serves 2
Takes 20 minutes

Soak the noodles in hot water for about 20 minutes until soft.

Butterflying the prawns helps them trap the spicy sauce. Cut along the length of each prawn, not quite all the way through, and pull out and discard the black vein (if you can see it).

Mix the cornflour and sriracha to a smooth paste, then stir in the ketchup and sweet chilli sauce with 3 tbsp water and some freshly ground black pepper.

When the noodles are nearly ready, heat the oil in a wok or frying pan. Add the prawns and fry until golden in places and curling up, then tip out of the pan. Add the onion, peppers and water chestnuts and stir-fry for a couple of minutes until the veg starts to colour. Stir in the garlic and ginger for a minute, then add the spicy sauce and prawns. Simmer fiercely for 2 minutes until thickened, then toss through the drained noodles and serve, topped with spring onions.

> **NOODLE SWAP:** boost your daily wholegrains by using flat brown rice noodles.

DUCK & HOISIN CHOW MEIN

DAIRY FREE

Ingredients

about 140g dried medium egg noodles (or 2 nests)

100ml hoisin sauce

3 tbsp Shaoxing rice wine or dry sherry

1 tbsp dark soy sauce

vegetable oil, for frying

175g stir-fry duck breast strips

75g mangetout

4 spring onions, cut into short lengths

2 garlic cloves, sliced

1 large pak choi or equivalent (baby pak choi or choi sum, etc.), leaves separated

If you can't find ready-prepared duck strips, simply pull and discard the skin from a large duck breast, then finely slice.

Serves 2
Takes 15 minutes

Boil the noodles until soft. Drain and leave in the sieve until you're ready for them.

Whisk together the hoisin sauce, rice wine or sherry and soy sauce.

Heat a splash of oil in a wok or large frying pan. Add the duck and stir-fry for 1–2 minutes until almost cooked, then tip out onto a plate. Wipe out the pan with kitchen paper, then add a splash more oil with the mangetout, spring onion and garlic. Stir-fry for 2 minutes. Add the pak choi leaves and stir-fry for a minute more.

Tip the hoisin sauce mixture into the pan – it should bubble immediately. Quickly add the noodles and toss with the saucy vegetables for a minute, then tip in the duck and any juices too. Toss together for another minute until the noodles are hot and the duck cooked to your liking.

NOODLE SWAP:
try udon.

CRISPY FRIED NOODLES WITH CHICKEN, CHILLIES AND HOLY BASIL

DAIRY FREE

Ingredients

100g dried medium or thick egg noodles

2 garlic cloves, peeled and halved

1 red chilli, trimmed but not deseeded

1 onion, sliced

2 small or 1 large chicken breast, sliced

125g green beans, trimmed

2 tbsp oyster sauce

1 tbsp light soy sauce

1 tsp fish sauce

1 tsp caster sugar

small handful of Thai basil leaves

If the crispy noodle cake seems a step too far, this is equally delicious tossed simply with soft noodles.

Serves 2
Takes 30 minutes

Boil the noodles for 3–4 minutes until tender. Rinse and drain, then tip onto kitchen paper or a clean tea towel to dry really well. Heat 2 teaspoons of flavourless oil in a small frying pan over a medium-low heat. Swirl to coat the base and sides, then add the noodles and use a potato masher to press down into an even cake. Fry, without moving, for 4–5 minutes until the base is crisp, golden and set. Carefully invert the pan onto a plate and turn out the noodle cake so the crispy base is on top. Keep warm under foil or in a low oven while you stir-fry the chicken.

Whizz the garlic cloves and whole chilli with another tablespoon of oil in a mini food processor. Scrape into a wok or large frying pan and sizzle for a minute. Add the onion for 30 seconds, followed by the chicken and beans, and stir-fry for 2 minutes. Drizzle over the oyster, soy and fish sauces and add the sugar and 2 tbsp water. Bubble the sauce fiercely, stirring constantly, until reduced and sticky and the chicken is glazed and cooked through. Take off the heat, fold through the Thai basil leaves and spoon over the crispy noodle cake for sharing.

> **NOODLE SWAP:**
> fine egg noodles work just as well for noodle cakes.

CHINESE CHILLI BEEF & BLACK BEAN PAN-FRY

DAIRY FREE

Ingredients

2 onions, 1 roughly chopped and 1 thinly sliced

125g black bean sauce

50g Chinese chilli or chilli-garlic sauce

2 fat garlic cloves

3 tbsp tomato purée

400g beef mince

200g green beans, trimmed

400g fresh or straight-to-wok medium egg noodles

1 tbsp dark soy sauce

This is an addictive umami overload – it's quite simply impossible to have leftovers.

Serves 4
Takes 40 minutes

Make a sauce by putting the chopped onion into a food processor with the black bean sauce, chilli sauce, garlic and tomato purée. Add 200ml water and whizz to a fairly smooth sauce.

Fry the beef in ½ tbsp oil in your largest frying pan, breaking up lumps with a wooden spoon as it browns. Tip the browned beef out onto a plate, and add the sliced onion with another ½ tbsp oil and a splash of water. Lower the heat slightly, and fry the onion until softened, scraping up any stuck beefy bits as you go. Return the beef to the pan, then stir in the sauce with another 200ml water. Bring to a simmer and cook for 15 minutes, stirring occasionally and scraping the bottom to stop it catching.

Cook the beans for 4 minutes in boiling water until tender, then drain. Carefully stir the beans, noodles and soy sauce through the beef mixture (if the pan is too full you can simply heat the noodles following the packet instructions then serve the beef on top). When the noodles are evenly mixed through and hot, serve.

NOODLE SWAP: almost any thin noodle will work well, just like spaghetti and Bolognese.

SWEET & SOUR AUBERGINES

VEGETARIAN + EGG AND DAIRY FREE

Vegan option: replace the honey with maple syrup

Ingredients

1 large aubergine, cut into 2cm chunks

100g dried medium wheat noodles

2 tsp cornflour

1 tbsp light soy sauce

1 tbsp dark soy sauce

1 tbsp tomato purée

3 tbsp rice vinegar

4 tsp runny honey

1 red onion, diced

Way better than a takeaway, this homemade sweet and sour sauce really packs a punch – and squishy aubergine is the perfect sauce-soaking vegetable to suck it all up!

Serves 2
Takes 30 minutes

Preheat the oven to 200°C/180°C fan/gas 6. Toss the aubergine with a tablespoon of oil in a shallow baking tray. Roast for 20 minutes until the aubergine is browning and soft.

Meanwhile, boil the noodles until tender, then drain.

Put the cornflour into a jug and mix in the light soy sauce to a smooth paste. Gradually stir in the dark soy, followed by the tomato purée, vinegar and honey.

Heat a small frying pan or wok with a teaspoon of oil and fry the onion for a few minutes until soft.

When the aubergine is ready, tip into the wok with the onion and the jug of sauce. Stir in 150ml water and bring the sauce to the boil over a high heat. Simmer until the sauce has thickened and reduced by about half, and is clinging to the vegetables. Rinse the noodles with hot water from the kettle to reheat, divide between two plates and top with the sweet and sour aubergines.

> **NOODLE SWAP:**
> 250g fresh egg noodles.

EGG-FRIED NOODLES WITH CHAR SIU PORK

DAIRY FREE

Ingredients

1 pork fillet, trimmed of fat

250g dried egg noodles

6 garlic cloves, thinly sliced

1 bunch of spring onions, white and green
 parts separated and sliced

3 tbsp vegetable or sunflower oil

200g frozen peas

3 eggs, beaten with a fork

4 tsp light soy sauce

For the marinade

125ml hoisin sauce

2 tbsp tomato ketchup

1 tbsp honey

1 tbsp dark soy sauce

The pork marinade and resulting sticky serving sauce is so moreish no one would question you making double… Marinate the pork for as long as you've got, but ideally overnight.

Serves 4–5
Takes less than 45 minutes + marinating

Mix together the marinade ingredients and season with ground black pepper. Coat the pork fillet, in a dish or food bag, and leave for as long as possible.

Preheat the oven to 220°C/200°C fan/gas 7. Remove the pork, reserving the marinade, and roast on a wire rack over a roasting tin for 18 minutes. Turn the oven down to 180°C/160°C fan/gas 4 and roast for a further 15 minutes. Check the pork is cooked through by cutting into the thickest part – if it's too pink, put back in the oven for another 3 minutes. Heat the marinade in a small saucepan until bubbling, then reduce for a few minutes until thickened. Boil the noodles at the same time until tender, then drain.

For the noodles, fry the garlic and spring onion whites in the oil until the garlic slices are golden. Stir in the peas, then push to one side of the pan. Pour the beaten eggs into the space, then scramble, stirring. Once just set, tip in the noodles and spring onion greens and toss together to mix thoroughly and heat the noodles up. Sprinkle over the soy sauce.

Thickly slice the pork and drizzle with the reduced marinade, then serve with the egg-fried noodles.

> **NOODLE SWAP:**
> no boiling required if you use fresh egg noodles instead.

MISO FRIED GREENS WITH UDON NOODLES

VEGAN

Ingredients

150g thin-stemmed broccoli
175g dried udon noodles
2 tsp sesame oil
4 spring onions, cut into thirds
150g sugar snap peas or mangetout
2 tsp toasted sesame seeds

For the dressing

4 tsp brown miso paste
1 tbsp rice vinegar, plus 2 tsp for the noodles
1 tbsp mirin, plus 1 tsp for the noodles
1 garlic clove, crushed

To up the protein you could add some tofu or black beans in with the vegetables, while a chopped red chilli on top adds an extra spicy kick.

**Serves 2
Takes less than 25 minutes**

Blanch the broccoli for 1 minute in a saucepan of boiling water – time from when the water begins to boil again. Drain and leave in the sieve until you start to stir-fry.

Mix together the dressing ingredients.

Fill another saucepan with water and bring to the boil. Add the noodles for about 4 minutes until tender. Heat a wok with the sesame oil and 1 tsp flavourless oil. Add the broccoli, spring onions and sugar snaps and stir-fry for 2–3 minutes until the veg starts to brown.

Drain the noodles and toss with the 2 teaspoons of vinegar and 1 of mirin. Divide between two plates and top with the stir-fried veg. Drizzle half the dressing over each and scatter with the sesame seeds.

NOODLE SWAP:
try soba.

SOULFUL SOUPS

BRILLIANT BEEF PHO

COCONUT ROAST SQUASH & KALE LAKSA

SLOW COOKER POACHED CHICKEN PHO

THAI YELLOW COD & COCONUT NOODLE

YAKI UDON WITH MUSHROOMS & SWEET SOY BROTH

HOT-SOUR SEAFOOD BROTH

FULL ENGLISH RAMEN WITH BACON BROTH

THAI GREEN SWEETCORN

CHILLI-MISO & KIMCHEE

BRILLIANT BEEF PHO

Ingredients

- 150g dried flat ribbon noodles, cooked following the packet instructions, cooled and drained.
- 1 litre beef stock
- 1 onion, thinly sliced
- 1 thumb-sized piece of ginger, sliced but no need to peel
- 2 star anise
- 2 tsp coriander seeds
- black peppercorns
- 1 small fillet or rump steak, trimmed of fat
- 1½ tbsp soy sauce
- 2 tsp fish sauce
- 1 tsp brown sugar (palm if you have it)
- 2 handfuls of soft herbs – a mixture of coriander, mint and Thai basil

Once you've mastered the basic recipe, this herb-topped classic can be tweaked according to your tastes – try adding fresh chilli and lime juice.

Serves 2
Takes 40 minutes

Put the stock, onion, ginger, star anise, coriander seeds and a few black peppercorns in a lidded saucepan. Place over a very low heat so the stock infuses as it comes to the boil – this might take up to 20 minutes. Once the broth is boiling, pop the lid on and simmer for 10 minutes.

Meanwhile, put the steak in the freezer for 15 minutes to help firm it up, then slice as thinly as possible with your sharpest knife. Divide between two big bowls with the drained noodles.

Strain the broth into a jug – you want 600–700ml for two servings. If there's not enough, top up with boiling water; too much, boil to reduce a little. Then use the soy sauce, fish sauce and sugar to season – it may need a splash more saltiness or a pinch more sweetness according to how you like it. Pour between the bowls – the heat from the broth will cook the beef. Serve scattered with the herbs.

> **NOODLE SWAP:**
> keep it classic with dried flat rice noodles.

COCONUT ROAST SQUASH & KALE LAKSA

Ingredients

1 small butternut squash, peeled and deseeded

3 tbsp desiccated or shredded coconut

4 tbsp korma paste

2 lemongrass stalks, snapped a few times down the length

8 kaffir lime leaves

1 x 400ml tin coconut milk

1 vegetable stock cube, crumbled

1 ball stem ginger, roughly chopped

50g kale leaves, weighed after removing the thick stalks, roughly chopped

pinch of sugar, to taste (optional)

100g flat brown rice noodles, cooked following the packet instructions

Ready-made laksa pastes usually contain fish sauce or shrimps, so put a Malay twist on a basic korma paste instead to keep this strictly veggie – and even vegan.

Serves 4
Takes 35 minutes

Preheat the oven to 220°C/200°C fan/gas 7. Halve and thickly slice the trunk end of the squash and space on an oiled baking tray, brushing the tops with a bit more oil. Season with salt and pepper and roast for 20 minutes, then carefully turn the slices – they'll be soft. Sprinkle with the desiccated coconut and bake for 2–3 minutes more until it has toasted. Dice the rounded end of the squash.

While the squash is roasting, put the curry paste, lemongrass stalks and lime leaves in a deep, lidded saucepan with 1 tbsp oil. Fry over a low heat for 3–4 minutes until fragrant – but don't let the mixture burn on the bottom. Pour in the coconut milk, then three tins of water (1.2L), and drop in the diced squash, stock cube and ginger. Bring to the boil. Pop on the lid and simmer for 10 minutes until the squash is tender. Fish out the lemongrass stalks, and use a handheld blender to whizz to a smooth soup.

Drop in the kale to blanch for a minute then check the seasoning – you might want to add a pinch of sugar, and some salt and pepper. Divide the noodles and soup between bowls and top with the roasted squash pieces.

NOODLE SWAP: flat rice noodles or udon – chunky veg goes with chunky noodles.

SLOW COOKER POACHED CHICKEN PHO

DAIRY AND EGG FREE

Ingredients

1 small whole chicken (approx. 1.5kg)

1 leek, roughly chopped

1 celery stick, roughly chopped (keep any leaves to serve)

1 thumb-sized piece of ginger, sliced

2 tsp coriander seeds

2 star anise

200g dried flat rice noodles

1 x 225g tin bamboo shoots, drained

To serve

1–2 chillies (any colour), sliced

4 spring onions, sliced on the diagonal

1 red onion, very thinly sliced (on a mandolin if you have one)

2 handfuls of coriander leaves

sauces of choice

For extra goodness, add some rice vinegar or apple cider vinegar to the chicken broth while it cooks. Acidity helps to extract even more healthy minerals from the chicken bones.

Serves 6
Takes all day but only 20 minutes of effort

Put the slow cooker on the low setting, add the chicken and cover with water if there's room; otherwise, cover as much as possible. Add the leek, celery, ginger, coriander seeds, star anise and 2 tsp salt and cook for 8 hours.

Lift the chicken from the broth and leave until it is cool enough to handle. Soak the noodles in boiling water until soft, then rinse under hot water and drain. Sieve the broth into a saucepan to keep warm.

Discard the skin and bones from the chicken and shred the meat. Stir into the broth with the noodles, bamboo shoots and some salt and pepper. Serve with small bowls of fresh chilli, spring onions, red onion, coriander and celery leaves (if you have them) for topping – plus your favourite sauces for drizzling in.

> **NOODLE SWAP:**
> try chewy ramen noodles.

THAI YELLOW COD & COCONUT NOODLE SOUP

`DAIRY AND EGG FREE`

Ingredients

2 tsp Thai yellow curry paste

1 tsp ground turmeric

1 x 400ml tin light coconut milk

4 round shallots, thinly sliced

about 10 coriander sprigs, leaves and stalks separated

100g frozen edamame beans

1 x 150g sachet straight-to-wok udon noodles

100g green beans, trimmed and halved

200g meaty white skinless fish, cut into chunks

1–2 limes

1 red chilli, thinly sliced

This soup is fairly substantial and makes a great supper dish – particularly served with a wedge of toasted naan bread on the side.

Serves 2
Takes 20 minutes

Whisk the curry paste, turmeric and coconut milk together in a large saucepan. Add 3 of the shallots and the coriander stalks – roughly chopped – with 400ml water. Bring to the boil, then simmer for 5 minutes. Use a handheld blender to whizz everything to a smooth broth.

Add the edamame and block of noodles, and once the broth has begun simmering again, add the beans and fish with the juice of 1 lime. Cook for 3–4 more minutes until the fish is cooked through – it is ready when it flakes easily when pressed.

Check the soup for seasoning – it'll need salt and maybe some more lime juice. Top with the remaining shallot slices, the red chilli and the coriander leaves. Any leftover lime can be cut into wedges and served alongside.

NOODLE SWAP:
rice vermicelli or flat noodles.

YAKI UDON WITH MUSHROOMS & SWEET SOY BROTH

VEGAN

Ingredients

1 onion, finely sliced

2 tsp sesame oil

125g chestnut mushrooms, sliced

1 x 300g packet mixed stir-fry vegetables

300g straight-to-wok udon noodles

4 tbsp dark soy sauce

4 tbsp kecap manis

4 tbsp oyster sauce

1 tbsp sesame seeds

If you've got any old veg to use up, why not shred 300g of mixed vegetables rather than buying a ready-prepared stir-fry packet?

Serves 4
Takes 10 minutes

Gently fry the onion in the sesame oil in a deep saucepan. When the onion is almost soft, stir in the mushrooms and cook for a minute.

Tip the stir-fry vegetables and udon noodles into the pan with 900ml water. Add both soy sauces and the oyster sauce, then bring to the boil. Simmer for 2–3 minutes until the veg is cooked through but still retains a bit of bite. Ladle between bowls and scatter with the sesame seeds.

NOODLE SWAP:
soba – just soak first.

HOT-SOUR SEAFOOD BROTH

DAIRY AND EGG FREE + GLUTEN FREE

Ingredients

6 king prawns with shells on

450ml chicken or fish stock

6 kaffir lime leaves

1 thumb-sized piece of ginger, sliced

2 red chillies, 1 halved lengthways, 1 sliced

50g dried rice vermicelli noodles

½ small onion, thinly sliced

150g mixed fish or seafood – e.g. salmon, white fish and squid rings

6–8 oyster mushrooms

2–3 tsp fish sauce

juice of 2 limes

3 tbsp chopped coriander

You can simply use peeled prawns for ease, but the shells add lots of fishy richness to the broth.

Serves 2
Takes less than 30 minutes

Pull the heads from the prawns and discard, then peel off the shells. Put the shells in a saucepan with the stock, lime leaves, ginger and halved chilli. Bring to the boil, then simmer gently for 5 minutes before leaving to stand for another 10 minutes.

Soak the vermicelli noodles until tender, then rinse and drain.

Fish the prawn shells, lime leaves and ginger out of the stock. Scatter in the sliced onion and bring back to the boil, before turning down to a low simmer. Cut the fish into bite-size pieces and add to the soup with the peeled prawns and mushrooms. Cook gently for 4–5 minutes until all the fish is cooked. Season with 2 teaspoons of fish sauce and half the lime juice, then taste. It will probably need some more lime, and maybe another teaspoon of fish sauce, depending on how strong you like it. Add the coriander to finish.

Divide the noodles between two bowls then ladle the fish and broth over the top.

NOODLE SWAP: try black noodles or glass noodles for an even more delicate dish.

FULL ENGLISH RAMEN WITH BACON BROTH

DAIRY FREE

Ingredients

7 streaky bacon rashers

6 chestnut or similar mushrooms, sliced

packet of instant shoyu (soy sauce) ramen to serve 2

3 spring onions, sliced

a little brown sauce, to taste, plus extra to serve (optional)

2 Jammy eggs (see page 14), halved

To serve

hot chilli sauce

furikake seasoning or sesame seeds

Like a full English in a bowl … of noodles. Up the vitamins? Add a handful of spinach leaves or frozen peas towards the end – or both – and get your iron and vitamin C hit in one go.

Serves 2
Takes less than 20 minutes

Cook the bacon in a deep frying pan with a dash of oil. When both sides are browned and crispy lift onto kitchen paper to drain off the excess oil.

Add the mushrooms to the pan and fry in the residual oil for a couple of minutes. Make up the ramen noodles following the packet instructions, but in the mushroom-filled pan. When you add the flavouring sachet, break in 3 of the crispy bacon rashers too.

When the noodles are ready, stir in most of the spring onions and a little brown sauce according to taste. Divide the ramen between bowls, adding 2 crispy bacon rashers to each and topping with the jammy eggs. Scatter over the remaining spring onions and serve with a drizzle of spicy sauce, a sprinkling of furikake seasoning, and some extra brown sauce too if you fancy.

> **NOODLE SWAP:**
> look for different ramen flavours like tonkatsu or miso.

THAI GREEN SWEETCORN SOUP

DAIRY FREE + EGG FREE + GLUTEN FREE

just check the curry-paste ingredients

Ingredients

2 tbsp Thai green curry paste

5 spring onions, white and green parts separated and finely chopped

1 x 400ml tin light coconut milk

1 vegetable stock cube

350g sweetcorn kernels, frozen, fresh or tinned (drained)

zest and juice of 1 lime

½ tsp caster sugar

2 tsp fish sauce

75g green beans, trimmed and diced

85g dried rice vermicelli noodles

This soup keeps well for a few days in the fridge, so it's ideal for packed lunches.

Serves 4
Takes less than 20 minutes

Combine the curry paste, spring onion whites, coconut milk, stock cube, 150g of the corn and 500ml water in a large, lidded saucepan. Bring to a simmer then blitz with a handheld blender. Add the lime juice, sugar, fish sauce, remaining sweetcorn and green beans.

Bubble for 3–4 minutes until the green beans are cooked. Stir in the noodles and lime zest, then turn off the heat, cover and leave for 3–4 minutes until the noodles are tender. Serve in bowls with the spring onion greens scattered on top; or if you're making a batch for the week just stir the greens through.

> **NOODLE SWAP:**
> medium wheat noodles.

CHILLI-MISO & KIMCHEE SOUP

DAIRY FREE

Ingredients

50g dried ramen noodles

1 sachet miso soup

2 tsp chilli oil

3 tbsp kimchee

50g tofu, diced

1 Jammy egg (see page 14), halved

1 nori sheet, snipped into strips

chilli flakes, to serve (optional)

If you're vegan simply skip the jammy egg and get your protein from the tofu instead.

Serves 1
Takes less than 15 minutes

Cook the noodles following the packet instructions, then drain and put into a deep bowl.

Make up the sachet of miso paste with the recommended quantity of water in a small saucepan. Add the chilli oil, kimchee and tofu and simmer for a couple of minutes to heat through.

Pour the miso–tofu soup over the noodles and top with the jammy egg. Scatter with nori strips and a pinch of chilli flakes if you want it spicier.

NOODLE SWAP:
udon noodles.

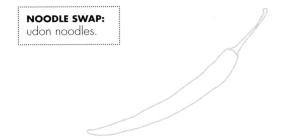

COMFORTING CURRIES

FISH FINGER KATSU UDON

MIDWEEK RED CURRY WITH ROOTS

FRIDAY NIGHT CURRIED SINGAPORE NOODLES

RAISUKAREE CHICKEN & EDAMAME

SRI LANKAN CURRIED KOTTU
WITH NOODLES

15-MINUTE KOREAN CHICKEN

CURRIED COCONUT NOODLE BOWLS

PULL-APART BEEF RENDANG
WITH GOLDEN NOODLES

BALINESE

PEANUT BUTTER PUMPKIN
WITH CRISPY NOODLES

FISH FINGER KATSU UDON

DAIRY FREE + EGG FREE + GLUTEN FREE

if you buy gluten-free fish fingers

Ingredients

8–12 good-quality fish fingers
(depending on how hungry you are)
600g straight-to-wok udon noodles

For the curry sauce

2 onions, thinly sliced
2 carrots, scrubbed and thinly sliced
½ apple, peeled and thinly sliced
1 garlic clove, crushed
1 tbsp ginger paste
4 tsp mild curry powder
1 tsp ground turmeric
1 x 400ml tin light coconut milk

To serve

a few sesame seeds or handful of
coriander
1 cucumber, thinly sliced
lemon wedges

*Posh fish fingers make for a fab cheat's katsu – and
if you batch-cook plenty of the sauce, you'll always
have a great dinner lying in wait in the freezer.*

Serves 4
Takes less than 40 minutes

Make the sauce by gently cooking the onions, carrots and
apple together in a deep, lidded frying pan in 1 tbsp oil.
When they're soft and the onions are starting to turn golden,
stir in the garlic and ginger paste for a minute. Stir in the spices
and give them another minute to toast, then pour in the coconut
milk. Rinse out the tin by half-filling with water and pouring in
too. Simmer, covered, for 20 minutes, then purée to a smooth
sauce with a blender. Season well with salt and pepper and
pour back into the pan.

Cook the fish fingers and noodles following the packet
instructions. Warm the sauce through, and bubble until nice
and thick if it's a little thin. Add the hot udon noodles and toss
together to thoroughly coat. Top the curried noodles with crispy
fish fingers and a sprinkling of sesame seeds or coriander, and
serve with the cucumber slices on the side and lemon wedges
for squeezing over.

NOODLE SWAP:
anything robust works well, so the thicker the better.

MIDWEEK RED CURRY WITH ROOTS

VEGAN

just check the curry paste

Ingredients

3 red onions, cut into wedges

400g carrots, peeled and cut into large chunks

400g parsnips, peeled, cored and cut into large chunks

500g sweet potatoes or butternut squash, peeled and cut into large chunks

200g dried wholewheat or medium wheat noodles

a few coriander leaves or snipped chives, to serve

For the sauce

1 x 400g tin chopped tomatoes

1 litre fresh coconut drink (milk alternative made with rice milk)

3 tbsp Thai red curry paste

2 tsp ground turmeric

juice of ½ lemon, plus wedges to serve (optional)

This tomatoey Thai curry uses clever tricks to achieve an impressive result with minimal effort.

Serves 4–5
Takes less than 45 minutes

Preheat the oven to 200°C/180°C fan/gas 6. Toss the onions and carrots with 1 tbsp olive oil and season with salt and pepper in a big roasting tin. Roast for 5 minutes, then stir in the parsnips, sweet potatoes or squash and roast for 25 minutes until all the veg is tender and browning around the edges.

While the veg is roasting, tip the tomatoes, coconut-rice drink, curry paste and turmeric into a deep saucepan. Bring to the boil, then lower the heat slightly and simmer for 20 minutes until the sauce is thickened and reduced by about half. Season with the lemon juice, then some salt and pepper.

Boil the noodles following the packet instructions. Drain well.

Divide the noodles between wide serving bowls and top with the roasted veg. Spoon over some sauce, scatter with the green herbs and serve with lemon wedges for squeezing over if you like.

NOODLE SWAP:
flat rice noodles, white or brown.

FRIDAY NIGHT CURRIED SINGAPORE NOODLES

DAIRY AND EGG FREE

Ingredients

100g dried rice vermicelli noodles

2 tbsp light soy sauce

1½ tbsp Shaoxing rice wine or dry sherry

2 tsp mild curry powder

pinch of sugar

1 onion, chopped

2 garlic cloves, sliced

200g diced leftover vegetables – peppers, carrots, broccoli, spring onions, mushrooms, cabbage are all good

100–125g ham, diced, or prawns, or a mixture

Clear out the fridge (and freezer) of all your week-night leftovers for the weekend ahead – and make a tasty, fakeaway-style dinner at the same time. To serve, just add a fork, a sofa and a box set.

Serves 2
Takes less than 15 minutes

Soak the noodles in boiling water. Drain well and leave in the sieve while you prepare the sauce.

Dry out the bowl the noodles were soaking in, then add the soy sauce, rice wine and half the curry powder and whisk together. Season with a good pinch of sugar. Tip in the noodles and toss to coat.

Heat a splash of oil in a wok or non-stick frying pan. Soften the onion over a medium heat, then stir in the garlic with the remaining curry powder. Stir and cook out the spices for a minute.

Increase the heat under the pan and tip in the vegetables. Stir-fry for a couple of minutes, then add the ham/prawns and the noodles. Use a spatula to scrape out every last drop of the sauce from the bowl. Toss everything together for a couple of minutes to mix thoroughly, then serve.

NOODLE SWAP:
this classic deserves the traditional choice.

RAISUKAREE CHICKEN & EDAMAME CURRY

EGG AND DAIRY FREE
just check the curry paste

Ingredients

12 skinless, boneless chicken thighs

3 tbsp Thai yellow curry paste

2 onions, diced

2 tbsp medium curry powder

2 x 400ml tins full-fat or light coconut milk

2 tbsp sweet chilli sauce

4 large peppers (any colours), cut into bite-size chunks

300g frozen edamame beans

1 tbsp cornflour

zest and juice of 2 limes

400g dried soba noodles

1 tbsp black sesame seeds

Look for a curry powder containing turmeric for a good, golden finish – failing that, add in an extra teaspoon with the spices. Putting the coconut milk in the fridge the night before ensures good separation.

Serves 6
Takes just over 1 hour

Fry the chicken thighs in a big, lidded casserole pan with a tablespoon of the yellow curry paste and a dribble of oil. Don't worry about browning the chicken – you just want all the pieces sealed and not raw-looking. Remove the chicken to a plate.

Add the onions to the casserole with another small spoonful of oil. Soften for 5–8 minutes then stir in the remaining curry paste and the curry powder. Open the tins of coconut milk and spoon the solid tops into the pan. Fry together for a few minutes until fragrant, but stop if the mixture starts sticking. Tip in the rest of the coconut milk along with 2 tinfuls of water and the chilli sauce, and bring to a simmer.

Return the chicken to the pan then cover and simmer gently for 30 minutes. Add the peppers, increase the heat, remove the lid and cook for 15 minutes. Mix 1–2 tablespoons of the sauce with the cornflour and mash to a smooth paste, then stir in enough extra sauce to loosen. Stir back into the curry and let it bubble again while stirring – the sauce will thicken up. Season with salt, pepper, the lime zest and as much juice as you need.

Cook the edamame beans in a small pan of boiling water for 5 minutes and in a separate pan cook the noodles for 4 minutes in boiling, salted water. Put the kettle on so that as soon as the noodles are ready you can rinse with the hot water to remove all the starch, then drain. Serve the noodles topped with the curry and scattered with sesame seeds and the edamame beans.

NOODLE SWAP: flat brown rice noodles – just as good at sucking up sauce but gluten free.

SRI LANKAN CURRIED KOTTU WITH NOODLES

VEGETARIAN

Ingredients

100g dried wholewheat noodles

1 large carrot, thinly sliced on the diagonal

100g hunk of white cabbage, shredded

knob of butter

1 large egg, beaten with a fork

1 onion, diced

2 garlic cloves, chopped

2 medium tomatoes, diced

10 curry leaves, fresh or dried

4 tsp mild curry powder

1 lemon

1 tbsp light soy sauce

big handful of coriander leaves, roughly chopped

This Sri Lankan classic is made with leftover roti bread or what are known as 'string hoppers' – hard to find in the UK, but most closely resembling thin brown noodles.

Serves 2
Takes less than 40 minutes

Boil the noodles until just about tender but still with a good amount of bite, then drain.

Heat 2 tsp oil in a wok or non-stick frying pan, then stir-fry the carrot and cabbage for 3–4 minutes. Push the vegetables to one side of the pan and drop the butter in the space before pouring in the egg. Lightly scramble, stir through the veg, then tip the whole lot onto a plate. Wipe the pan with some kitchen paper.

Pour a mugful of water (approx. 250ml) into the same pan with the onion, garlic, tomatoes, curry leaves and curry powder. Fry, stirring occasionally, until you have a saucy curry paste and the onion is soft. Stir in the juice of half the lemon and the soy sauce and fry for another minute, then gently fold through the drained noodles and eggy veg – try not to smush everything together too much. When piping hot, take the pan off the heat and fold through the coriander and season with salt and pepper. Cut the remaining lemon half into wedges and serve on the side in case you need a squeeze more.

> **NOODLE SWAP:**
> skinny soba for a gluten-free option.

15-MINUTE KOREAN CHICKEN CURRY

`EGG FREE + DAIRY FREE`

Ingredients

- 2 tbsp gochujang paste
- 2 tsp cornflour
- 1 large skinless chicken breast, cut into strips
- 1 tsp freshly grated ginger
- 200ml light coconut milk
- 1 tbsp dark soy sauce
- 1 tsp palm or light brown soft sugar
- 150g dried ramen or medium wheat noodles
- 100g green beans, trimmed
- 150g frozen peas or edamame beans
- 2 spring onions, chopped

Curries don't get any quicker and easier than this one!

Serves 2
Takes 15 minutes

Stir together the gochujang and cornflour to a smooth paste.

Heat 2 tsp oil in a non-stick frying pan or wok and stir-fry the chicken and ginger. When the chicken is sealed – it doesn't need to be browned – stir in the gochujang and cornflour paste, followed by the coconut milk, soy sauce and sugar. Simmer for 8–10 minutes until the chicken is tender and the sauce has thickened.

Meanwhile, bring a saucepan of water to the boil. Add the noodles and boil for 2 minutes, then drop in the beans, peas or edamame, and spring onions. Boil for another 2 minutes, then drain and serve with the chicken curry.

> **NOODLE SWAP:**
> try udon.

CURRIED COCONUT NOODLE BOWLS

CAN BE VEGETARIAN + DAIRY AND EGG FREE

Ingredients

300g straight-to-wok ribbon rice noodles

1 tbsp coconut oil

4 tsp mild curry powder

2 green chillies, 1 deseeded and finely chopped, 1 thinly sliced

200ml light or full-fat coconut milk

200ml chicken or vegetable stock

600g mixed ready-spiralised veg – try courgetti and butternut-squash 'boodles'

200–250g protein of choice – see introduction above

1 tbsp light or dark soy sauce

1 tbsp hot-sweet chilli or regular sweet chilli sauce

To serve

a few roasted cashews or peanuts

coriander or mint leaves

toasted coconut or Homemade crispy fried onions (see page 15; or use ready-made)

This is a great recipe for using up the contents of your fridge – good with shredded leftover chicken, diced tofu, prawns or even cooked meatballs.

Serves 4
Takes less than 25 minutes

Put the noodles in a sieve then pour over a kettle of boiling water – this helps to loosen them up for stir-frying.

Melt the coconut oil in a wide frying pan. When it starts to sizzle, tip in the curry powder and chopped chilli. Fry for a minute, then add the coconut milk and stock. When bubbling, throw in the spiralised veg. Keep tossing and turning the vegetables through the sauce for a couple of minutes, then add in the noodles plus the protein of your choice.

Fry everything together for 2–3 minutes, until the whole lot is piping hot, then season with the soy sauce and chilli sauce. Divide between four bowls and top with the sliced green chilli and any favourites from the serving suggestions.

NOODLE SWAP: look for other vegetable noodles (sweet potato or carrot, for example) in the supermarket to vary your spiralised veg.

PULL-APART BEEF RENDANG WITH GOLDEN NOODLES

DAIRY AND EGG FREE + GLUTEN FREE

Ingredients

1.2kg best stewing beef (weighed after trimming of fat), cut into big chunks

1½ onions, diced

2 star anise

1 x 160ml tin coconut cream

1 chicken stock pot

200–250g dried flat rice noodles

1 tsp light brown or other sugar

handful of coriander leaves, to serve

For the curry paste

1½ onions, chunkily sliced

2 lemongrass stalks, roughly chopped

4 garlic cloves

1 large red chilli, deseeded

1 thumb-sized piece of ginger, peeled and roughly chopped

1 tbsp each brown mustard seeds, coriander seeds and ground turmeric

This fragrant curry takes a while to cook, but the method is reassuringly easy. The long cooking time ensures that the meat is melt-in-the-mouth succulent and delicious. This dish is also good made with diced lamb leg, so give that a try too.

Serves 4–5
Takes less than 5 hours – mostly cooking time

To make the paste, put the onions in a food processor with the lemongrass, garlic, chilli, ginger, mustard and coriander seeds. Add 1 teaspoon of the turmeric and half a mug of water (around 125ml) and whizz to a smooth paste.

Heat 1 tbsp oil in a deep, lidded casserole pan and brown the beef chunks – in batches if that's easier. Remove all the meat to a plate, and tip in the onions with a mug of water (around 250ml). Fry until all the stuck beef bits have bubbled up into the onions and they're softening. Add the paste and continue frying for about 5 minutes – the paste should be fragrant and darkening.

Preheat the oven to 160°C/140°C fan/gas 3.

Return the beef to the casserole with the star anise and coconut cream. Stir in enough water to just cover all the beef, and when it comes to a simmer, cover and put in the oven. Cook for 3–4 hours until the beef is really tender and falling apart, and the sauce has thickened and reduced. Cooking times will vary depending on the cut of beef.

Put 2L water in a big saucepan with the remaining turmeric and the stock pot. Bring to the boil then add the noodles and cook for 2–3 minutes until tender. Rinse with hot water from the kettle and drain.

Season the curry with salt, pepper and the sugar. Scatter with the coriander leaves and serve with the golden noodles.

> **NOODLE SWAP:** anything robust to hold its own against the beef. Udon or chewy soba would also be good.

BALINESE CURRY

Ingredients

100g dried flat rice noodles

1 onion, roughly chopped

1 red chilli, deseeded

75g roasted cashews

2 tsp ground turmeric

2 tsp tamarind paste

1 lemongrass stalk, roughly chopped

zest of 1 lime

200ml light coconut milk

400ml chicken stock

2 skinless chicken breasts

250g mixed frozen vegetables

If you can't be sitting on a sunny beach right now, you can at least cook food that makes you think you are. This fragrant curry uses coconut, cashews, lime and tamarind to bring all the flavours of the tropics.

Serves 2
Takes 35 minutes

Soak the noodles in hot water until soft, then rinse with hot water and drain.

Meanwhile, put the onion, chilli, 50g of the cashews, the turmeric, tamarind, lemongrass and lime zest in a mini food processor. Pour in 4 tbsp water and whizz to as smooth a paste as possible. (If necessary, add a tablespoon more water.)

Fry the paste in a deep, lidded saucepan for 3–4 minutes until fragrant. If it starts to stick, turn down the heat. Stir in the coconut milk and chicken stock, then add the chicken. Bring to a gentle simmer, then cover and cook for 10 minutes over a low heat. Fish out the chicken breasts to slice. Stir in the frozen vegetables and simmer for 5–10 minutes, uncovered, until the sauce is creamy. Add the chicken slices, stir and leave on the heat for a minute if they weren't totally cooked through.

Towards the end, toast the remaining cashews in a small frying pan then roughly chop. Stir the noodles through the curry and serve, scattered with the toasted cashews.

> **NOODLE SWAP:**
> wholewheat noodles for extra fibre.

PEANUT BUTTER PUMPKIN CURRY WITH CRISPY NOODLES

`VEGETARIAN + DAIRY FREE`

Ingredients

1 litre sunflower oil, for deep-frying

150g fresh or straight-to-wok medium egg noodles

350g round shallots, peeled and trimmed

125g crunchy peanut butter

2 tbsp tomato purée

2 balls stem ginger, grated, plus 1 tbsp of the syrup

2 tbsp light soy sauce

5 tbsp lime juice

150ml coconut cream

800g hunk sweet pumpkin (e.g. Delica or Crown Prince) or butternut squash, peeled, deseeded and cut into big chunks

100g spinach leaves

¼ tsp red pepper powder or chilli flakes (to serve)

For the coriander relish

small bunch of coriander

This is a pretty smart-looking curry that's great for entertaining – add some jasmine or basmati rice to serve, if you like.

Serves 4
Takes less than 45 minutes

Fill a high-sided wok or saucepan with oil to a depth of 8–10cm. When a cube of bread dropped in the oil immediately starts bubbling fiercely, you're ready to fry. Line a tray with kitchen paper, then use metal tongs to carefully add a small bunch of noodles at a time to the hot oil, frying for 10–20 seconds until pale golden and crispy. Drain on the kitchen paper.

Bring 1L water to the boil in a large saucepan, add the shallots and, once boiling again, cook for 4 minutes. Lift out the shallots with a slotted spoon.

Whisk the peanut butter, tomato purée, grated ginger and syrup, soy sauce, 2 tablespoons of the lime juice and the coconut cream into the saucepan of water. Bring the broth back to a simmer, then return the shallots with the pumpkin and simmer for 15 minutes until the vegetables are tender and the sauce has thickened. Stir through the spinach and season with salt and pepper.

To make the relish, whizz the whole coriander bunch, stalks and all, with the remaining 3 tablespoons of lime juice, 1 tbsp water and 1 tbsp oil, to a loose pesto texture in a small food processor.

Serve the curry in deep bowls, scattered with crispy noodles and topped with a spoonful of the coriander relish and a sprinkle of red pepper powder.

> **NOODLE SWAP:** these egg noodles are the perfect type for deep-frying.

Pimp To The Max Specials

BANG BANG CHICKEN SUMMER ROLLS

CRISPY FISH BANH MI WITH SHORTCUT
PICKLED VEG

CORN & CORIANDER NOODLE CAKES

WASABI, AVO & NOODLE SALAD WITH
SESAME-COATED SALMON

NOODLE-WRAPPED PRAWNS WITH
SWEET-SOUR CHILLI DIP

THAI LARB LETTUCE CUPS

NASI GORENG NOODLES WITH FRIED EGGS

SALMON & UDON OKONOMIYAKI

HAINANESE CHICKEN NOODLES

MISO-SOY-GLAZED MEATBALLS WITH
SOBA SALAD

BANG BANG CHICKEN SUMMER ROLLS

GLUTEN FREE + DAIRY AND EGG FREE

Ingredients

100g dried rice vermicelli noodles

12 large (20cm) round rice paper wrappers

1 large carrot, peeled and cut into fine matchsticks

1 courgette, cut into fine matchsticks

150g cooked chicken breast, finely shredded

12 coriander sprigs, stalks only

For the bang bang dipping sauce

75g smooth peanut butter

1 tbsp light soy sauce

2 tbsp sweet chilli sauce

juice of 1 lime

1 red chilli, deseeded and finely chopped

2 tbsp roasted peanuts, roughly chopped

Once you've mastered the technique, you can make these rolls with any fillings you like, and vary the dipping sauce to match.

Makes 12 rolls (share between 4 as a starter, 2 for dinner)
Takes 1 hour

Make the bang bang dipping sauce first: put 3 tbsp water and all the ingredients except the chilli in a mini food processor or blender. Whizz to a smooth sauce then add the chopped chilli and peanuts.

Soak the noodles in a bowl of hot water for 15 minutes, then rinse with cold water and drain well, before gently patting dry with kitchen paper.

To assemble the rolls, you will need a clean board, clean tea towel and wide bowl of hot water. Dip one rice paper wrapper in the water at a time, soaking it for 10–15 seconds until soft, then drain briefly on the tea towel. Lay on the board and along one edge place some carrot and courgette strips (you can use cucumber instead of courgette but deseed first to stop the rolls getting soggy), followed by some chicken, then a few noodles. Lay a coriander stalk on top, then roll up as tightly as you can. Don't overfill or it will be hard to roll up. When you get halfway, fold in the ends so the filling is completely enclosed. Repeat to make 12 rolls – don't worry if there's leftover filling.

Eat dunked generously in the dipping sauce.

NOODLE SWAP:
try glass noodles instead.

CRISPY FISH BANH MI WITH SHORTCUT PICKLED VEG

Ingredients

2 part-bake baguettes

2 tsp white or black sesame seeds

50g dried rice vermicelli or glass noodles

250g skinless, firm white fish

25g plain flour

¼ tsp ground turmeric

½ tsp ground coriander

3–4 tbsp mayonnaise

1 quantity Shortcut pickled veg (see page 14)

small handful of mint leaves

handful of coriander leaves

Vietnamese banh mi baguettes are layered with so many textures and flavours, they put most other sandwiches to shame! This crispy fish version is paired with soft, fine rice noodles and plenty of crunchy veg.

Serves 2
Takes less than 25 minutes

First, brush the tops of the baguettes with a little oil and sprinkle with the sesame seeds before cooking according to the packet instructions. Soak the noodles in hot water until tender, then rinse, drain and tip onto kitchen paper to dry really well. This will stop you ending up with a soggy sandwich.

Cut the fish into big chunks – just narrower than the baguette width. Tip the flour onto a plate, season with salt and pepper and stir in the turmeric and coriander. Add the fish chunks and roll around to coat.

Heat a splash of oil in a non-stick frying pan. When hot, add the fish a few chunks at a time. When one side is golden and crisp, use a spatula to carefully turn, until all sides are golden and crisp and the fish is cooked through.

Split the warm baguettes in half both ways, so you have two short, open baguettes for each person. Spread with the mayo, then make a base of noodles along one side. Top with the pickled vegetables, draining off excess pickle juice as you add them. Put the crispy fish chunks on top with some mint and coriander leaves. Sandwich each baguette half back together and eat straight away.

> **NOODLE SWAP:**
> thin noodles really work best.

CORN & CORIANDER NOODLE CAKES

VEGETARIAN

Ingredients

50g dried wholewheat noodles

100g plain flour

2 large eggs

1 tbsp milk

1 tsp baking powder

¼ tsp ground turmeric

1 tbsp sweet or hot-sweet chilli sauce, plus extra to serve

150g sweetcorn, frozen, fresh or tinned (drained)

handful of coriander leaves, 1 tbsp chopped

2 handfuls of mixed salad leaves

2 spring onions or small shallots, thinly sliced

1 avocado, diced

squeeze of lime or lemon juice

These moreish cakes make for a generous dinner, or they'd feed three or four for brunch, topped with poached eggs. You could even make mini versions and serve as a starter or canapés.

Serves 2 for dinner (makes 8–9 fritters)
Takes 30 minutes

Soak the noodles in hot water for about 20 minutes until tender, then rinse well and drain. Spread onto a few sheets of kitchen paper to dry well.

Whisk the flour, eggs, milk, baking powder, turmeric and chilli sauce to a smooth batter in a mixing bowl. Season with salt and pepper, then stir in the corn and chopped coriander. Put a kitchen-paper-lined baking tray in a low oven to keep warm.

When you're ready to cook, heat a non-stick frying pan with a shallow layer of oil. Snip the noodles a few times with kitchen scissors to shorten their length and stir into the batter – they'll absorb the batter gradually so are best mixed in at the last minute. Spoon roughly half the batter into four big fritters and fry for 2–3 minutes on one side until you can see bubbles in the batter on the top, then carefully flip. Cook for 2–3 minutes on the other side until the fritters are golden, then lift onto the prepared baking tray and keep warm while you cook the rest. Add a splash more oil if you need to.

Toss the rest of the coriander leaves with the salad leaves, the spring onions or shallots and avocado. Dress with a squeeze of lemon or lime juice and serve with the fritters, along with a good glug more sweet chilli sauce.

NOODLE SWAP:
dried medium wheat noodles.

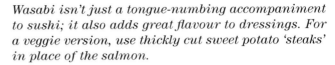

WASABI, AVO & NOODLE SALAD WITH SESAME-COATED SALMON

`DAIRY FREE`

Ingredients

2 salmon fillets

1–2 tbsp kewpie (Japanese) or regular mayonnaise

4 tbsp mixed black and white sesame seeds

125g dried green tea noodles

2 spring onions, finely sliced on the diagonal

1 ripe avocado

For the wasabi noodle dressing

1 tsp wasabi paste (or ½ tsp for flavour but no heat!)

zest and juice of 1 lime

1 spring onion, roughly chopped

½ small bunch of coriander, plus extra to serve

1 tbsp water

Wasabi isn't just a tongue-numbing accompaniment to sushi; it also adds great flavour to dressings. For a veggie version, use thickly cut sweet potato 'steaks' in place of the salmon.

Serves 2
Takes 25 minutes

First prepare the salmon by brushing the fish all over with the mayonnaise – just skip the skin side. Tip the sesame seeds onto a plate and roll each fillet in the seeds to thoroughly coat the skinless sides, then place on a baking tray skin-side down and preheat the oven to 220°C/200°C fan/gas 7.

Soak the noodles in a bowl of boiling water to soften.

Put the baking tray in the oven and bake the salmon for 8 minutes until just cooked through.

Put the dressing ingredients with 1 tbsp oil in a mini food processor and whizz to a pesto-like dressing.

Rinse the noodles with cold water, then drain and pat dry with kitchen paper and put into a bowl with the dressing. Add the sliced spring onions and toss to mix. Quickly slice the avocado and serve alongside the noodles. Serve with the sesame-coated salmon alongside.

NOODLE SWAP:
try other Japanese noodles such as soba.

NOODLE-WRAPPED PRAWNS WITH SWEET-SOUR CHILLI DIP

`DAIRY FREE`

Ingredients

50g dried medium egg noodles

16 coriander leaves

16 king prawns with shells, peeled but tails left on

1 litre vegetable oil, for frying

For the dipping sauce

3 tbsp caster sugar

5 tbsp rice vinegar

1 red chilli, deseeded and finely diced

3cm piece of carrot, finely diced

1 small round shallot, finely diced

5cm piece of cucumber, deseeded and finely diced

1 tsp sesame seeds

These might be a little fiddly, but they're easily prepared ahead and look really impressive once fried.

Serves 4
Takes 45 minutes + frying

Boil the noodles for 3–4 minutes until soft, then drain and quickly pat dry so they stick to the prawns more easily.

Lay a coriander leaf on each prawn before wrapping with 3–5 noodles to roughly lengthen the body. Leave the tail free. Once all the prawns have been wrapped in this way, put them in the fridge while you make the dipping sauce.

Put the sugar, vinegar, chilli, carrot and shallot in a small saucepan with 2 tbsp water. Heat gently until the sugar has completely dissolved. Tip into a shallow serving bowl and stir in the cucumber and sesame seeds. Season with a little salt.

Heat the oil in a deep wok or deep but narrow saucepan until a noodle thrown in browns in about 20 seconds. Fry 3–4 prawns at a time until the noodles are crisp and pale golden and the prawns are pink – 20–30 seconds. Lift out onto kitchen paper to drain while you fry the rest. Serve straight away, with the dipping sauce for dunking.

> **NOODLE SWAP:** wheat noodles of a similar thickness will work – even soba for their sticky properties.

THAI LARB LETTUCE CUPS

GLUTEN FREE + EGG AND DAIRY FREE

Ingredients

50g dried glass noodles

6 small round or 2–3 long shallots, peeled and roughly chopped

½ small bunch of coriander, leaves and stalks separated

½ lemongrass stalk

1 garlic clove

2 tsp fish sauce

1 tsp light brown sugar

400g turkey mince

2 baby gem or 1 romaine lettuce, leaves separated

1 lime, cut into wedges

If Laos had a national dish it would definitely be larb – a type of meat salad. Serving the tasty turkey and noodle fry in lettuce cups also makes it great sharing food, and this recipe is very easily doubled if friends come round.

Serves 2 generously
Takes 20 minutes

Soak the noodles until soft, then rinse and drain.

Put the shallots, coriander stalks, lemongrass, garlic, fish sauce and sugar in a mini food processor. Pulse to finely chop everything then scrape into a frying pan with the turkey mince and 1 tbsp oil. Fry, stirring constantly and using a wooden spoon to break up the mince as you do, until the turkey is golden and cooked through. Remove from the heat.

Arrange the lettuce leaves on plates or a platter and chop the coriander leaves. Snip the noodles a few times with a pair of kitchen scissors to make it easier to serve, then stir through the turkey with the coriander. Spoon the turkey–noodle mixture into the lettuce cups, and serve with lime wedges for squeezing over and your favourite sauces on the side.

> **NOODLE SWAP:**
> try rice vermicelli noodles or fine egg noodles.

NASI GORENG NOODLES WITH FRIED EGGS

DAIRY FREE

Ingredients

1 skinless chicken breast, diced

2 long or 4 round shallots, thinly sliced

100g extra-fine green beans, diced

1 large red chilli, sliced

2 tbsp nasi goreng spice paste

300g fresh or straight-to-wok medium egg noodles

1 tbsp kecap manis, plus extra to serve

1 tbsp light soy sauce, plus extra to serve

3 eggs, 1 beaten with a fork

To serve

2 tbsp Homemade crispy fried onions (see page 15) or ready-made

cucumber and tomato slices

prawn crackers

In Indonesia this classic dish, traditionally made with fried rice, is served for breakfast, brunch or lunch – and always accompanied by slices of cucumber and tomato. Our noodle twist makes a great dinner for two hungry people.

Serves 2
Takes less than 25 minutes

Heat a splash of oil in a wok or large frying pan and stir-fry the chicken for 2 minutes, then tip out onto a plate. Add a splash more oil with the shallots, green beans and half the chilli, and stir-fry for 2–3 minutes until the beans are tender. Return the chicken to the pan, then stir in the spice paste and cook for a further minute.

Turn down the heat and add the noodles with the kecap manis and soy sauce. Stir-fry for 2 minutes to heat the noodles through, then push everything to one side, leaving a small space to scramble the beaten egg. Pour in the egg, leave to set a little, then toss through the other ingredients in the pan. Take off the heat and cover with a lid or baking sheet to keep warm while you fry the remaining eggs to your liking in a splash of oil in a non-stick pan.

Quickly divide the nasi goreng noodles between two plates and arrange a fried egg on top of each. Scatter with the rest of the sliced chilli and the crispy onions, then arrange the cucumber and tomato slices alongside. Serve with prawn crackers and extra kecap manis and soy sauce for drizzling over.

> **NOODLE SWAP:**
> straight-to-wok flat rice noodles for a gluten-free alternative.

SALMON & UDON OKONOMIYAKI

`DAIRY FREE`

Ingredients

2 large eggs

100g plain flour

75g straight-to-wok udon noodles

50g sweetheart or white cabbage, finely shredded

2 spring onions, finely sliced

50–75g hot smoked salmon (or leftover cooked salmon), flaked into chunks

To serve

a little mayonnaise

brown sauce or Tonkatsu sauce (see page 15)

sushi ginger

Okonomiyaki is a Japanese savoury pancake filled with whatever seafood and veg you like. In fact, okonomi literally means 'what you like' in Japanese.

Serves 1–2
Takes less than 20 minutes

Whisk the eggs and flour with 125ml water (or 8 tablespoons) and some salt and pepper to make a smooth batter.

Boil the kettle, put the noodles in a sieve and pour over enough water to loosen the strands – they're normally stuck together until warmed (alternatively, just heat following the packet instructions).

Fold the cabbage, most of the spring onions, salmon chunks and noodles through the batter. Heat 1 tbsp oil in a small frying pan, about 20cm wide. Pour the mixture into the pan and press down to flatten – a spatula or potato masher works well. Cook for 5 minutes over a medium heat, then use a spatula or palette knife to carefully release the omelette and flip over. If it's easier, flip out of the pan onto a plate, then slide it back into the pan. Cook the other side for 5 minutes until golden and cooked through to the middle.

Slide the omelette onto a plate and drizzle with some mayonnaise and the brown or tonkatsu sauce. Scatter with the remaining spring onions and eat with sushi ginger.

> **NOODLE SWAP:**
> soaked and drained soba noodles.

HAINANESE CHICKEN NOODLES

`EGG FREE`

Ingredients

1 small whole chicken (about 1.4–1.5kg)
100g fresh ginger, sliced
5 spring onions, 3 sliced, 2 halved
6 peppercorns
250g dried flat rice noodles
2 tbsp butter
1 tbsp toasted sesame seeds
1 cucumber, peeled into ribbons
100ml soy sauce
100ml sesame oil

This is traditional Chinese comfort food of the highest order. Normally served with jasmine rice, this recipe's noodle twist puts a new spin on an otherwise classic dish.

Serves 4–6
Takes 1 hour and 15 minutes, plus standing and cooling time

Put the chicken in a large, lidded pot or saucepan and add enough water to ensure it is totally covered. Remove the chicken for the time being, but add the ginger and halved spring onions with the peppercorns and bring to the boil over a medium heat. Meanwhile, rub the chicken inside and out with 2 tsp salt. When the water is boiling, add the chicken. Cover and bring back to a rapid boil, then simmer for 10 minutes before lifting the pan off the heat and leaving to stand for 1 hour. Check the chicken is cooked by piercing the thickest part of the thigh and making sure the juices run clear. Cut away the breasts and keep in a bowl with a little of the stock. Put the pot with remaining chicken back on the heat and, once boiling again, simmer, uncovered, for 5 minutes. Cool again then lift out the rest of the chicken, carve into portions and keep moist with a little of the cooking water.

Soak the noodles until half-soft – about 20 minutes in cold water, then drain well. Tip into a frying pan with the butter and 400ml of the chicken stock. Fry, stirring, until the noodles are tender and the stock has almost gone. Stir through the sliced spring onions and sesame seeds and tip onto a serving platter. Arrange the chicken portions on another platter, and the cucumber ribbons on a third. Mix the soy and sesame oil together and spoon over the chicken portions as you serve.

> **NOODLE SWAP:**
> brown rice noodles for a super-healthy supper.

MISO-SOY-GLAZED MEATBALLS WITH SOBA SALAD

`DAIRY AND EGG FREE`

Ingredients

400g turkey mince

400g pork mince

2 tbsp brown or white miso paste

500g soba noodles

2 tbsp sesame oil

2 tbsp furikake seasoning

3 handfuls of baby kale, lamb's lettuce or other baby leaves

For the sauce

100ml dark soy sauce

100ml mirin

3 tbsp soft brown sugar

50ml rice vinegar, plus 1 tbsp extra for the noodles

Homemade meatballs are a guaranteed crowd pleaser. If entertaining, add the Shortcut pickled veg (see page 14) and some sushi ginger to serve alongside too.

Serves 5–6
Takes 45 minutes

Mix the turkey and pork mince together with the miso paste, season with salt and pepper and roll into about 30 meatballs. Put in the fridge to firm up while you preheat a big baking tray in the oven at 200°C/180°C fan/gas 6.

To make the sauce, put all the ingredients in a large frying pan and mix together over a gentle heat. Once the sugar has dissolved, take off the heat.

Soak the noodles for 15–20 minutes in hot water.

Carefully drizzle a little cooking oil into the preheated baking tray, add the meatballs and roll around to coat. Bake for 10 minutes.

Transfer the meatballs to the frying pan with the sauce. Cook over a medium heat, keeping a close eye once the sauce begins to boil, stirring and turning the meatballs constantly to stop them sticking. When the sauce is looking really glossy, thick and sticky, and the meatballs are well glazed, take off the heat.

Once soft, rinse the soba noodles well with cold water, then drain and tip onto a clean tea towel to mop up any excess water before transferring to a serving dish. Drizzle over the sesame oil and extra tablespoon of vinegar and toss through the noodles with the furikake seasoning. Lightly mix through the leaves. Serve the sticky, glazed meatballs and sauce on the side.

NOODLE SWAP: go really glam with half soba, half black rice noodles.

INDEX

apple
Chinese shredded duck, clementine & noodle salad 33
Fish finger katsu udon 75
Shredded cabbage, apple & miso slaw 34
aubergine
Sweet & sour aubergines 54
avocado
Avo-topped tahini 25
Corn & coriander noodle cakes 93
Crunchy veg goodness bowl with eggs 38
Wasabi, avo & noodle salad with sesame-coated salmon 94

bacon
Full English ramen with bacon broth 69
Marmite butter & bacon 19
bean, black
Noodle omelette roll-ups 22
bean, edamame
15-minute Korean chicken curry 81
Raisukaree chicken & edamame curry 79
Super-green noodle salad with tahini dressing 30
Thai yellow cod & coconut noodle soup 65
bean, green
15-minute Korean chicken curry 81
Chinese chilli beef & black bean pan-fry 52
Crispy fried noodles with chicken, chillies and holy basil 51
Nasi goreng noodles with fried eggs 99
Thai green sweetcorn soup 70
Thai som tam salad with swede & glass noodles 31
Thai yellow cod & coconut noodle soup 65
Thai-style watermelon, green bean & cashew salad 41
beef
Brilliant beef pho 61
Chinese chilli beef & black bean pan-fry 52
Pull-apart beef rendang with golden noodles 84
broccoli
Crunchy veg goodness bowl with eggs 38
Miso fried greens with udon noodles 56
butternut squash
Coconut roast squash & kale laksa 62
Curried coconut noodle bowls 82
Midweek red curry with roots 76
Peanut butter pumpkin curry with crispy noodles 86

cabbage
Crunchy veg goodness bowl with eggs 38
Salmon & udon okonomiyaki 100
Satay chicken noodle salad 29
Shredded cabbage, apple & miso slaw 34
Sri Lankan curried kottu with noodles 80
chestnut, water
Chinese shredded duck, clementine & noodle salad 33
Firecracker prawn noodles 48
chicken
15-minute Korean chicken curry 81
Balinese curry 85
Bang bang chicken summer rolls 90
Crispy fried noodles with chicken, chillies and holy basil 51
Hainanese chicken noodles 101
Nasi goreng noodles with fried eggs 99
Noodle omelette roll-ups 22
Raisukaree chicken & edamame curry 79
Satay chicken noodle salad 29
Slow-cooker poached chicken pho 63
clementine
Chinese shredded duck, clementine & noodle salad 33
coconut
Coconut roast squash & kale laksa 62
Curried coconut noodle bowls 82
courgette
Bang bang chicken summer rolls 90
Curried coconut noodle bowls 82
Pork patties with Vietnamese noodle salad 35
crab
Green mango & rice noodle salad with crab 36

duck
Chinese shredded duck, clementine & noodle salad 33
Duck & hoisin chow mein 50

egg
Chilli-miso & kimchee soup 71
Crunchy veg goodness bowl with eggs 38
Egg-fried noodles with char siu pork 55
Full English ramen with bacon broth 69
Jammy eggs 14
Salmon & udon okonomiyaki 100
Sri Lankan curried kottu with noodles 80

fish, see also crab, prawn, salmon, squid
Fish finger katsu udon **75**
Hot-sour seafood broth **67**
Thai yellow cod & coconut noodle soup **65**

ham
Friday night curried Singapore noodles **77**

kale
Coconut roast squash & kale laksa **62**
Crunchy veg goodness bowl with eggs **38**
Miso-soy-glazed meatballs with soba salad **103**

mandarin
Chinese shredded duck, clementine & noodle salad **33**
mango
Green mango & rice noodle salad with crab **36**
Marmite
Marmite butter & bacon **19**
mushroom
Dan dan-don't noodles **47**
Full English ramen with bacon broth **69**
Hot-sour seafood broth **67**
Miso-mushroom & herb **20**
Yaki udon with mushrooms & sweet soy broth **66**

noodle (any)
Shaken-jar sriracha sauce **21**
noodle, black
Chinese shredded duck, clementine & noodle salad **33**
noodle, egg
Chinese chilli beef & black bean pan-fry **52**
Chinese shredded duck, clementine & noodle salad **33**
Crispy fried noodles with chicken, chillies and holy basil **51**
Duck & hoisin chow mein **50**
Egg-fried noodles with char siu pork **55**
Lemon, parmesan & pistachio **18**
Marmite butter & bacon **19**
Nasi goreng noodles with fried eggs **99**
Noodle-wrapped prawns with sweet-sour chilli dip **96**
Peanut butter pumpkin curry with crispy noodles **86**
Sweet soy salmon **23**

noodle, glass
Crispy fish banh mi with shortcut pickled veg **92**
Thai larb lettuce cups **97**
Thai som tam salad with swede & glass noodles **31**
noodle, green tea 94
Wasabi, avo & noodle salad with sesame-coated salmon **94**
noodle, Japanese
Tonkatsu sauce **15**
noodle, ramen
15-minute Korean chicken curry **81**
Chilli-miso & kimchee soup **71**
noodle, rice
Avo-topped tahini **25**
Balinese curry **85**
Brilliant beef pho **61**
Coconut roast squash & kale laksa **62**
Crowd-pleasing pad Thai **45**
Curried coconut noodle bowls **82**
Firecracker prawn noodles **48**
French onion pho **20**
Hainanese chicken noodles **101**
Pork patties with Vietnamese noodle salad **35**
Pull-apart beef rendang with golden noodles **84**
Satay chicken noodle salad **29**
Shredded cabbage, apple & miso slaw **34**
Slow-cooker poached chicken pho **63**
Super-green noodle salad with tahini dressing **30**
Thai-style watermelon, green bean & cashew salad **41**
noodle, rice vermicelli
Bang bang chicken summer rolls **90**
Crispy fish banh mi with shortcut pickled veg **92**
Friday night curried Singapore noodles **77**
Green mango & rice noodle salad with crab **36**
Hot-sour seafood broth **67**
Noodle omelette roll-ups **22**
Pork patties with Vietnamese noodle salad **35**
Thai green sweetcorn soup **70**
noodle, soba
Crunchy veg goodness bowl with eggs **38**
Miso-soy-glazed meatballs with soba salad **103**
Raisukaree chicken & edamame curry **79**
Roast sweet potato & salmon noodle salad **39**

noodle, udon
Buttered gochujang **24**
Dan dan-don't noodles **47**
Fish finger katsu udon **75**
Miso fried greens with udon noodles **56**
Salmon & udon okonomiyaki **100**
Thai yellow cod & coconut noodle soup **65**
Yaki udon with mushrooms & sweet soy broth **66**

noodle, vermicelli
Miso-mushroom & herb **20**

noodle, wheat
15-minute Korean chicken curry **81**
Midweek red curry with roots **76**
Sweet & sour aubergines **54**

noodle, wholewheat
Avo-topped tahini **25**
Corn & coriander noodle cakes **93**
Kimchee fried noodles **46**
Midweek red curry with roots **76**
Sri Lankan curried kottu with noodles **80**

pea
15-minute Korean chicken curry **81**
Egg-fried noodles with char siu pork **55**

pea, mangetout
Duck & hoisin chow mein **50**
Miso fried greens with udon noodles **56**

pea, sugar snap
Miso fried greens with udon noodles **56**
Super-green noodle salad with tahini dressing **30**

peppers (red/yellow, etc.)
Firecracker prawn noodles **48**
Kimchee fried noodles **46**
Raisukaree chicken & edamame curry **79**

pork (also see bacon, ham)
Egg-fried noodles with char siu pork **55**
Miso-soy-glazed meatballs with soba salad **103**
Pork patties with Vietnamese noodle salad **35**

prawn
Firecracker prawn noodles **48**
Friday night curried Singapore noodles **77**
Hot-sour seafood broth **67**
Noodle omelette roll-ups **22**
Noodle-wrapped prawns with sweet-sour chilli dip **96**

pumpkin
Peanut butter pumpkin curry with crispy noodles **86**

salmon
Avo-topped tahini **25**
Hot-sour seafood broth **67**
Noodle omelette roll-ups **22**
Roast sweet potato & salmon noodle salad **39**
Salmon & udon okonomiyaki **100**
Wasabi, avo & noodle salad with sesame-coated salmon **94**

spinach
Lemon, parmesan & pistachio **18**
Peanut butter pumpkin curry with crispy noodles **86**

squid
Hot-sour seafood broth **67**

swede
Thai som tam salad with swede & glass noodles **31**

sweet potato
Midweek red curry with roots **76**
Roast sweet potato & salmon noodle salad **39**

sweetcorn
Corn & coriander noodle cakes **93**
Thai green sweetcorn soup **70**

tofu
Chilli-miso & kimchee soup **71**
Crowd-pleasing pad Thai **45**

tomato
Midweek red curry with roots **76**
Nasi goreng noodles with fried eggs **99**
Sri Lankan curried kottu with noodles **80**
Thai som tam salad with swede & glass noodles **31**

turkey
Miso-soy-glazed meatballs with soba salad **103**
Thai larb lettuce cups **97**

vegetables, mixed
Balinese curry **85**
Friday night curried Singapore noodles **77**
Yaki udon with mushrooms & sweet soy broth **66**

vegetables, pickled
Crispy fish banh mi with shortcut pickled veg **92**
Shortcut pickled veg **14**